Prime Suspect

Deborah Jermyn

BFI

palgrave
macmillan

A BFI book published by Palgrave Macmillan

For Miranda

Images from *Prime Suspect*, © Granada Television; *Quincy, M.E.*, Glen A. Larson Productions/Universal TV; *The Silence of the Lambs*, Orion Pictures Corporation/Strong Heart/Demme; *Juliet Bravo*, BBC; *The Gentle Touch*, London Weekend Television.

Whilst considerable effort has been made to correctly identify the copyright holders, this has not been possible in all cases. We apologise for any omissions or mistakes in the credits and we will endeavour to remedy, in future editions, errors brought to our attention by the relevant rights holder.

None of the content of this publication is intended to imply that it is endorsed by the programme's broadcaster or production companies involved.

First published in 2010 by
PALGRAVE MACMILLAN

on behalf of the

BRITISH FILM INSTITUTE
21 Stephen Street, London W1T 1LN
www.bfi.org.uk

There's more to discover about film and television through the BFI. Our world-renowned archive, cinemas, festivals, films, publications and learning resources are here to inspire you.

Palgrave Macmillan in the UK is an imprint of Macmillan Publishers Limited, registered in England, company number 785998, of Houndmills, Basingstoke, Hampshire RG21 6XS. Palgrave Macmillan in the US is a division of St Martin's Press LLC, 175 Fifth Avenue, New York, NY 10010. Palgrave Macmillan is the global academic imprint of the above companies and has companies and representatives throughout the world. Palgrave® and Macmillan® are registered trademarks in the United States, the United Kingdom, Europe and other countries.

Set by Cambrian Typesetters, Camberley, Surrey
Printed in China

This book is printed on paper suitable for recycling and made from fully managed and sustained forest sources. Logging, pulping and manufacturing processes are expected to conform to the environmental regulations of the country of origin.

British Library Cataloguing-in-Publication Data

A catalogue record for this book is available from the British Library

ISBN 978–1–84457–305–9

Contents

Acknowledgments

Thanks first to Rebecca Barden, who commissioned this book at BFI Publishing and so helpfully supported its development; to the editors of the 'TV Classics' series, for their encouraging and constructive feedback on the proposal; and to Sophia Contento and Horst Sarubin for producing the frame grabs. I am particularly grateful also to Will Brooker and Stacey Abbott for their thoughtful reading of draft chapters, and to Su, for sharing my enthusiasm for *Prime Suspect* over the years and being at hand to consider my musings – it continues to be my great pleasure to play Watson to her Holmes. During the research for this book, Matt Wagner sat through many hours of DVDs when he would probably rather have been at the theatre. As always, I am indebted to him for his patience, encouragement and insightfulness and can only hope that one day I'll be able to tell him something useful about Shakespeare in return. Finally, this book is dedicated to our growing bump. Her/his increasingly insistent nudging during the writing of this book was a special motivation to keep working and a daily reminder that in the midst of the darkness the research for this volume inevitably touched on, a ray of light was waiting to meet us at the end.

Parts of Chapters 2 and 3 were previously published in 'Women with a Mission: Lynda La Plante, DCI Jane Tennison and the Reinvention of British TV Crime Drama', *International Journal of Cultural Studies* vol. 6 no. 1, March 2003, pp. 46–63.

Introduction: Locating the Evidence of a 'TV Classic'

The term 'water-cooler television' has become commonplace in popular vernacular over recent years in relation to memorable TV shows. It speaks to the manner in which some programmes break out of 'the flow' of television's everyday stream of sounds and images to enter our cultural consciousness in exceptional ways. Such shows can give rise to new language, spark discussion about our beliefs and values, move us and prompt us to think in ways that stay with us. When we speak of 'water-cooler television' we acknowledge how television can make itself felt widely outside 'the box' and outside our homes to become part of public life and debate, sometimes with lasting resonance.

When *Prime Suspect* was first broadcast on British television in April 1991, it quickly became apparent that just such a show had arrived. At the time I was a student living in the Midlands, and I can still remember the sensation of being in the midst of a national TV 'moment'. The morning after the first instalment was shown, it seemed like everyone wanted to know if you'd seen it. Those hideous dead bodies! Helen Mirren in a TV crime show! A killer who was, well, unnervingly normal (wasn't he?). Audiences were captivated as the resilient, career-driven Detective Chief Inspector Jane Tennison (Mirren) pursued a serial killer with a penchant for raping and torturing his victims, while fighting too for her own survival in the chauvinistic world of the police. The press applauded the show's revelatory performances and storyline and eagerly anticipated its conclusion. *Time Out*, for example, heralded the ITV miniseries police procedural as 'a belter of a suspense thriller', bringing an inventive twist to the staple cop-show format by conceiving a female detective who was 'a masterpiece of observation and subtlety'.[1] Overnight *Prime Suspect* became one of the most talked-about British TV programmes in recent memory, giving rise, as Philip Purser noted in the *Daily Telegraph*, to a nation 'united, divided, mesmerised, offended and generally caught up in a television whodunnit'.[2] The term 'water-cooler television' may still have been a while off entry into popular discourse in 1991, but it is here in spirit in Purser's summary. How exactly did *Prime Suspect* achieve this status, and create one of television's most celebrated and contentious woman protagonists? Why, in fact, is *Prime Suspect* worthy of inclusion in the book series to which this volume belongs, as a programme warranting recognition as a 'TV Classic'? In addressing these questions, this book examines exactly what made *Prime Suspect* stand out from the crime-drama crowd to become such an inventive, controversial and, ultimately, influential instance of one of television's most consistently popular and longest-standing genres.

Even the most cursory glance through the pages of a typical TV guide today points to the ubiquity of television crime drama on contemporary screens. In recent years in particular, *CSI: Crime Scene Investigation* (CBS, 2000–) has become the most successful television franchise of all time and throughout TV history, crime dramas have featured as reliable 'bankers' for broadcasters seeking to ensure regular, return audiences. But TV genres, like their filmic counterparts, cannot remain static. If they are to avoid becoming stale and overly predictable they must periodically be reimagined, bringing new character types, settings, themes or aesthetics to bear. It is in this process of generic evolution that, occasionally, a 'TV Classic' emerges.

In what follows I argue that *Prime Suspect* was responsible for instigating major changes to TV crime drama, entailing shifts which would have a lasting impact on the police series and which ensured that in its wake the genre moved in directions hitherto only glimpsed. When the first instalment of *Prime Suspect* aired, the sheer originality of a female cop as driven and yet as nuanced as Tennison took audiences and critics well used to the conventions and overwhelmingly male heroes of the cop show by surprise.[3] While there had of course been women detectives and female cops before, not merely on television but in literature and cinema, Tennison was a highly distinctive addition to their number, combining feminine instinct with cool forthrightness. Her signature line would become the blunt directive, 'Don't call me ma'am, call me guv'nor or boss', a command delivered repeatedly across the series as various colleagues try to undermine her authority and remind her of her difference from their other, male superiors.

In the original storyline, following the discovery of a woman's body in a London bedsit, we first meet Tennison at the start of the murder inquiry when she is pointedly overlooked for the case by her boss Detective Superintendent Kernan (John Benfield), despite having been on-call when it was reported. When the DCI leading the investigation, John Shefford (John Forgeham), unexpectedly dies of a heart attack while on the brink of charging his suspect, Tennison insists she should take over from him and eventually is grudgingly given the case. She is subsequently met with suspicion and non-cooperation by Shefford's (almost entirely male) team, particularly his close friend and ally, Detective Sergeant Bill Otley (Tom Bell), before she gradually wins them over with her undeniable dedication and skill. In contrast to Shefford's brash, slapdash style, she eventually builds a solid case against the 'prime suspect', the likeable and unassuming George Marlow (John Bowe), proving Shefford's misidentification of the first victim; revealing other murders in the north to have been Marlow's handiwork also; and 'breaking' Marlow's girlfriend, Moyra (a superbly textured performance by Zoë Wanamaker), into retracting her alibi – all while negotiating a cut-throat chauvinistic world which seeks to exclude and belittle her. The price she must pay for this success is her own relationship, however, and following one late night too many on the case, her weary partner Peter (Tom Wilkinson) moves out. By the end of

3

the investigation Tennison is left vindicated but alone, a scenario that will become all too familiar throughout the series that follow.

Tapping into the preoccupations of the day, in 1991 *Prime Suspect*'s exploration of police sexism constituted a particularly highly charged subject for a British crime drama. It coincided with the very public real-life tribunal of Merseyside's Assistant Chief Constable, Alison Halford, at the time the UK's senior woman police officer. Revelations about Halford having repeatedly been denied promotion due to sexual discrimination meant that the 'glass ceiling' of the police service for female officers and the prejudice they experienced were issues very much in the public mind. Mirren's portrayal of a woman battling to save her own name, as well as the lives of other women, perfectly captured the tensions and dilemmas at stake in such an environment. Relentlessly shot in contemplative and often unflattering close-up by

In the frame: as DCI Jane Tennison, Helen Mirren eschewed flattering camera angles and lighting

director Christopher Menaul, her chain-smoking 'virtuoso performance'[4] would win her some of the greatest acclaim of her career.

Crucially too, and all the more contentiously *because* the investigator at work was a woman, *Prime Suspect* included forensic sequences featuring graphic imagery and explicit detail that were a landmark in TV crime drama, and in the medium of television itself. The relentless close attention it paid to the victims' butchered bodies was unprecedented on the small screen and led to much press discussion, as well as complaints to the then Broadcasting Standards Council. Where cutaways and reaction shots were once the order of the day in crime drama, *Prime Suspect* did not flinch from showing the dead bodies, crime scenes and post-mortem photos of its victims. In fact, the early scene where Tennison first attends the morgue to see the body of Karen Howard can be read as a playful intertextual nod to the opening credits of the 1970s US crime show *Quincy, M.E.* (NBC, 1976–83). In this memorable sequence, the eponymous medical examiner (Jack Klugman) grandly tells the line of uniformed cops assembled in the morgue, 'Gentlemen, you are about to enter the most fascinating sphere of police work, the world of forensic medicine!' As he whisks back the sheet covering an unshown cadaver and gets to work, each of them faint away at the sight of the body in a series of reaction shots. It is a sequence that would be unimaginable in today's media culture, preoccupied as it is with making evidence visible for public inspection. At the vanguard of this new order, *Prime Suspect* observed none of *Quincy, M.E.*'s discretion: instead it repeatedly displayed the full horror of victims' battered corpses. In a rare moment of humour, Tennison's first visit to the morgue mocks any chauvinist presumptions the audience may hold when she asks where the bathroom is after inspecting Karen's body. As she turns to her junior male colleague, Jonesy (Ian Fitzgibbon), looking decidedly queasy next to her we realise *he* is the one about to make a hasty exit. In contrast, just like Quincy, Tennison's focus and professionalism is underlined by her ability to examine the body without flinching.

Such moments of forensic realism, while groundbreaking in 1991, have since become *de rigueur* in TV crime drama. Watching the

5

Quincy's row of rookie cops swoon as the unshown cadaver is revealed to them

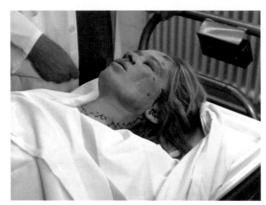

Prime Suspect swiftly displays the corpse's 'severe facial bruising' but it is Jonesy, not Tennison, who needs the bathroom as a result

6

first series' strangely contemplative 'behind-the-scenes' forays into the crime labs today it is striking how much *CSI* and its imitators are indebted to the sea-change that *Prime Suspect* initiated. Elsewhere too, an intimate exploration of the corpse and human remains has become commonplace in series such as *Silent Witness* (BBC, 1996–) or more recently *Bones* (Fox, 2005–). As these programmes also illustrate, the cultural turn towards forensics is often accompanied by a female investigator, interestingly presenting this kind of work as a legitimate 'feminine' pursuit.[5] But while driving such innovations *Prime Suspect* also demonstrated the apparent inexorability and limitations of TV crime drama, as a number of the cop show's habitual conventions remained firmly present. Tennison is just one in a long line of dedicated detectives seemingly forever doomed to battle internal hierarchies and sacrifice health and happiness to 'the job'. This familiar territory took on a whole new series of ramifications, however, when the cop in question was a woman.

Prime Suspect's original brilliance lay in the way it cleverly advanced a two-pronged narrative, examining the institution of the police itself at the same time as delivering a classically suspenseful thriller. Within this the drama centred both on Tennison's workplace battle for survival and the investigation's race to lock up a misogynistic serial killer, showing the issues at stake in each to be intricately entwined. Polite, amiable George Marlow, the likeable 'Everyman' under suspicion for the women's murders, is actually far less menacing than Tennison's nemesis, DS Otley, a detective who has little patience with the 'tarts' he has to deal with on the case. The resonances of such a murder inquiry would have been keenly felt among many UK audiences still conscious of the West Yorkshire Police's infamous mismanagement of the 'Yorkshire Ripper' case in the 1970s to early 1980s. In one of the UK's most notorious serial-killer investigations, thirteen women across northern England were murdered by Bradford lorry driver Peter Sutcliffe. The case prompted a major manhunt, later lambasted for the negligent manner in which police had investigated those victims who had worked as prostitutes. Amy Taubin's *Village Voice* review shrewdly

7

evoked the parallels between this real-life case and its fictional counterpart when she observed, 'The dramatic conflict in *Prime Suspect* is twofold: Tennison is up against both criminal and institutionalized hatred of women'.[6] On a further front, one might also add to this that she is 'up against' the history of the male-dominated crime series itself.

Later storylines would not centre on Tennison's battle with institutional sexism to quite the same degree, but the issue would continue to resurface throughout the series. By the time *Prime Suspect 2* is underway a year after the Marlow case, for example, her position initially appears far more assured than it had been. Otley has been transferred, she has a team who now know and respect her, and Kernan is apparently on-side at last, immediately appointing Tennison to head up a new case when the skeletal remains of a young woman are found buried at a local house. But as the drama develops, Tennison's marginalisation becomes evident again, this time in part signalled by the presence of another old boys' club within the police, the Freemasons. A new nemesis in the shape of DCI Thorndike (Stephen Boxer) emerges, as it becomes clear he has the ear of the area Commander and is out to undermine her. Tennison solves the case, but when Kernan is promoted to Detective Chief Superintendent her hopes of succeeding him are short-lived. Instead her promotion prospects are dashed as Thorndike wins Kernan's old job, not because he's better qualified, but because of his 'Lodge' connections.

While the problem of women's workplace exclusion would be revisited as the series progressed, *Prime Suspect* would build a reputation for grappling with other difficult and disquieting themes. Later series continued to tackle topical or 'taboo' social issues, from police racism and deaths in police custody in *Prime Suspect 2*; paedophilia, homeless rent boys and police homophobia in *Prime Suspect 3*; infanticide in *Prime Suspect 4: The Lost Child*; gang and gun culture in *Prime Suspect 5: Errors of Judgement*; to war crime and the disenfranchisement of the UK's refugee and immigrant communities in *Prime Suspect 6: The Last Witness*. As the series unfolded, what came to

Inside the boys' club: Tennison's bosses collude over drinks to block her promotion prospects

unify it across these diverse themes was a sceptical or ambivalent perspective on the ability of police work to satisfactorily deal with such issues. Tennison always solves the crime, but this, *Prime Suspect* suggests, is not to presume the case is closed or justice served. Loopholes, whitewashes and back-room dealings will always remain to be navigated in the world of modern policing. In *Prime Suspect 3*, for example, despite being continuously warned off her enquiries, Tennison successfully proves that a senior Met police officer, Assistant Deputy Commissioner John Kennington (Terence Harvey), is a paedophile who worked with social worker Edward Parker-Jones (Ciarán Hinds) to abuse boys in their care. She exposes the police cover-up that has protected them, but this is not sufficient to bring them to trial. Kennington commits suicide before an arrest can be made and Parker-Jones's lawyer gets him off without charge. To uncover the truth is not necessarily to entirely reach 'resolution' in the world of *Prime Suspect*.

Most dishearteningly of all, it is sometimes the police themselves who are an impediment to justice.

After a hiatus of seven years between *Prime Suspect 5* and *6*, the programme would eventually number seven miniseries broadcast over a period of some fifteen years, at last reaching its (controversial) conclusion in 2006 with *Prime Suspect: The Final Act*.[7] It would be fair to say the series had a somewhat uneven broadcast history, both in terms of the quality and regularity of its constituent parts. But regardless of the mixed reception which met some of the later series, each time Mirren reprised the role of Tennison her return was excitedly anticipated in the UK as 'event television'. Enthusiastically trailed by ITV and keenly awaited by television audiences and commentators, Tennison had become one of those rather rare television characters whose every appearance generated column inches, even winning the number one spot on Channel 4's *Top Ten TV: Cops* in September 2001. Mirren's performances helped establish Tennison as a landmark character – and not only one of the most significant *women* – in the history of crime drama, in the process bestowing 'national treasure' status on Mirren in the UK.

In no sense though was *Prime Suspect* a series that spoke only to British audiences. It gained worldwide distribution and in the US was broadcast from its inception on public television as part of the prestigious 'Masterpiece Theatre' series. Following the first miniseries it was produced by Granada in association with WGBH, the Boston-based non-commercial TV and radio broadcast service and leading producer of US PBS (Public Broadcasting Service) primetime programming. The fact that the ensuing acclaim was won by an ITV drama brought valuable kudos to this commercial channel. *Prime Suspect* confirmed ITV's capacity for producing 'quality' drama during a period when such standards were highly contested across British television, doing much to demonstrate that it could deliver original, thought-provoking and highly exportable programming. Filmed by turns to evoke the shadowy criminal world of film noir one moment and the starkness of a quasi-documentary the next, the first *Prime Suspect* established the series as one which was just as rich aesthetically as it was thematically. Looking more like a feature film than a TV cop show at times, its intermittent use of deep-focus photography and startling camera angles alongside its respected theatre- and film-star lead all underscored *Prime Suspect*'s standing as quality television.

In recognition of this, the series would go on to win numerous awards in the US, including three Emmys for 'Outstanding Miniseries' and two for 'Outstanding Lead Actress in a Miniseries or a Special'. Series creator Lynda La Plante would become known as one of the leading TV dramatists in Britain, winning BAFTAs for 'Best Drama Serial' in both 1992 and 1994. Over the course of its lifetime, as critics and fans argued in the press and on the Internet about whether Tennison should or shouldn't attain a happy home life, should or shouldn't make it to the top brass, should or shouldn't slip steadily into alcoholism, she would refuse to be bullied out of her profession. Instead she would go on to make the senior rank of Detective Superintendent, investigating a series of harrowing cases while fighting her own personal demons, losing lovers and family in the process, and somewhere along the way entering the annals of television history as a TV cop who broke the mould.

This book explores the processes this journey entailed. I examine La Plante's account of writing *Prime Suspect*; I trace the generic and televisual innovations of the programme and the evolution of Tennison in the context of the history of the cop show; and reflect on the legacy of the programme visible in the explosion of crime and forensic drama that has dominated our television landscape since the 1990s. Ultimately *Prime Suspect* achieved what television at its best aspires to, capturing and interrogating the cultural *Zeitgeist* of its day, delivering some unforgettable perfomances, while daring to rework the boundaries of one of television's most popular and enduring genres. Tennison may now have taken her final bow. An abundance of new female investigators may have taken to our screens. Dead and decaying bodies may have ceased to shock us as they once did and forensic jargon may have become our second language. But for reasons I will explore here, none of this would have been so without *Prime Suspect*.

11

1 Investigating the Evolution of *Prime Suspect*

There is a tradition within British television history of approaching our most celebrated shows and series as 'belonging' to the creative vision of one or two individuals. Typically, such an approach has elevated a (largely male) pantheon of screenwriters to auteur status. There is undeniably something romantic and appealing about this methodology which perpetuates the myth of 'the great artist' and brings this cachet to bear on a medium often looked down upon as the poor relation of cinema. And yet television production is in fact a highly collaborative creative endeavour, one best understood as evolving within a whole *web* of connected social and historical contexts. This includes the aspirations and talents of individuals but also the needs of the industry at any one time, as well as its textual and generic histories. It is with this latter approach in mind that this chapter discusses some of the creative forces, generic conventions and other contexts that were central to how the series came to be made. From writer Lynda La Plante to police consultant Jackie Malton and Tennison's fictional predecessors, together these interests form the 'back story' to *Prime Suspect*.

The Women Behind the Woman

While any simple 'auteur' approach to television falls short of fully grasping the medium, undeniably pre-eminent in the evolution of *Prime Suspect* was the actor-turned-writer who devised it, Lynda La Plante. The programme is still widely recalled as 'a Lynda La Plante series', though in fact she wrote only the first and third instalments.[8] Equally, it remains her most celebrated work, even though she has continued to be prolific since it was first broadcast as writer and producer of a range of primetime dramas, often featuring powerful women working in masculine milieux, including *The Governor* (1995–6); *Trial and Retribution* (1996–) and *The Commander* (2003–). In 1993 La Plante severed her ties with *Prime Suspect* under difficult circumstances after irresolvable creative differences with Granada emerged during the third series. These apparently centred on the direction Jane Tennison's character should take, since La Plante was insistent in the face of opposition at Granada that the series should not dedicate more screen time to Tennison's private life.[9] She had also become increasingly resentful of the fact that she was only a 'writer for hire' at Granada who did not 'own' *Prime Suspect* despite devising it, a situation that later prompted her to set up her own production company. Her departure was perhaps most clearly signalled by a shift in the narrative structure in series four, where the contemplative two x two-hour miniseries format was replaced by a more compacted three x two-hour self-contained episode format (*The Lost Child*; *Inner Circles*; *The Scent of Darkness*). It is interesting to note too that the work of those writers who followed La Plante was not met by anything like the same popular or critical attention. This seems in part because the later series did not (and could not hope to) reprise the degree of impact that the first had achieved. But beyond this, by the time La Plante left, *Prime Suspect* had developed into something bigger than any individual 'writer for hire', becoming a kind of brand inextricably bound up with its star, Helen Mirren. This is borne out by the fact of Mirren's increasing input into significant production decisions and developments. Mirren has even said, for

13

example, that the shift to a three x two-hour format in 1995 'was my responsibility. I thought it was time for a change'.[10]

This was not the first time La Plante had experienced the capricious world of television writing. Almost a decade earlier in 1983 she had enjoyed huge but short-lived success as the writer of *Widows*. Broadcast as a six-part serial on ITV (and followed by a rather less well-received sequel, *Widows 2*, in 1985), it followed a team of female robbers who pull off a heist together following the deaths of their criminal husbands during a botched security-van raid. Presaging the interest that would meet *Prime Suspect*, *Widows* won acclaim for taking a crime-genre staple – in this instance the heist drama – and shaking up its masculine traditions by reimagining it with a group of women at its core. In interviews explaining how she came to write *Widows*, La Plante

Former actor Lynda La Plante, writer of the original *Prime Suspect*

recurrently describes how she was driven by frustration at the lack of intelligent or complex roles open to her as a television actor. She reached a crossroads after appearing in the British police series *The Gentle Touch* (ITV, 1980–4) as 'Juanita', an improbably named East End prostitute encumbered with equally unlikely dialogue. Deciding that the only way to ensure better roles for women was to write them, La Plante submitted a number of draft scripts to the series' script editors. All were rejected, but one of them, 'The Women', containing a plot about a group of women married to a gang of robbers who carry out a robbery of their own, came back to her with the words 'This is brilliant' written across it.[11] Newly encouraged, she decided to develop the script for Euston Films instead, who already had a track record of successful crime dramas having made shows such as *The Sweeney* (ITV, 1975–8) and *Out* (Thames Television, 1978). On hearing her outline of 'The Women', script editor Linda Agran decided to commission La Plante to write the first part of *Widows* and to produce the series herself, and a landmark series was underway.

That *Widows* came to be made was not, however, merely the inspired result of La Plante's creative vision or disillusionment as an actress. Rather it emerged from a fortuitous meeting of like-minded individuals – more specifically, like-minded women, including Verity Lambert and Linda Agran at Euston Films – working in a production context that could facilitate the making of this apparently risky series. Each of the women involved was tired of the dearth of female protagonists on primetime television. They came together at a cultural and institutional moment which was ripe for tackling the gender imbalance in television, visible at the level of both representation and production. As Julia Hallam has argued, women in positions of authority in the British television industry were a rarity at this time.[12] The relatively large number of women instrumental in producing *Widows* was notable for this reason (and would be again when *Prime Suspect* was made). Among her peers Verity Lambert had therefore enjoyed quite exceptional success as a producer, rising in the early 1980s to become head of drama at Thames Television and executive producer of Euston Films. When La Plante approached Euston Films, Lambert

15

was already looking to address what she saw as the male-dominated focus of its productions. Prompted in part by 'feminist friends', she had become 'conscious of the fact that I really should try and do something about women'.[13] Lambert's reference to the influence of her 'feminist friends' speaks of the growing momentum of the women's movement over the preceding decade. The campaigning initiatives of 'second-wave feminism' did more than target changes in legislation, such as the Sex Discrimination Act of 1975. They also recognised the import of media representations and stereotypes in promoting prejudice, shoring up a burgeoning feminist critical interest in television. In this respect it was undeniably somewhat retrograde that *Widows'* only black protagonist had also to be a dominatrix-stripper and occasional prostitute. In other respects, though, *Widows* was ambitious, provocative material. Establishing themes that were to become characteristic of La Plante's writing, it also expanded the role of women in crime drama and primetime programming and in this sense it remains one of *Prime Suspect's* most significant precursors.

Following the acclaim that met *Widows*, it had seemed certain that La Plante's star would continue to rise. In fact, while she began to enjoy some success as a novelist, her TV writing career essentially stalled. Entering a hiatus that would not truly be broken until *Prime Suspect*, she has described how 'all everybody wanted was another *Widows* … I was writing all these scripts and storylines and everything was being turned down. It was a horrible time'.[14] When the opportunity arose to meet informally with script editor Jenny Sheridan from Granada, La Plante decided to take another approach:

> And this time I thought, 'Be clever. Ask her what projects they want'. And she said 'Well, we're really looking for a police drama'. And I said, 'Oh, I've got one of those'. Then she said 'But we want a woman leading role'. I said, 'Ah, it's strange you should say that because I do have a woman leading'. I just bullshitted my way through the interview and at the end of it she said 'Well, what's your police drama called?' and I said 'Prime Suspect'. I had never thought about the title. I didn't have a character, a plot, nothing.[15]

According to this anecdote, the germ of the idea that became *Prime Suspect* actually originated with Granada. Demonstrating the difficulty of accurately constructing television history, however, La Plante has contradicted this account in other interviews where she has recalled writing *Prime Suspect* after watching the BBC crime appeal programme *Crimewatch* (1984–) and noting its dearth of women officers.[16] The title that La Plante came up with under duress was conveniently enigmatic, lending itself to different interpretations. At one level it was satisfyingly generic, connoting the familiar, resolution-driven terrain of crime drama, indicating that the narrative will be propelled by the desire to identify, pursue and apprehend the guilty. But this reading only really works in respect of the first series, which follows Tennison's criminal antagonist, George Marlow, more doggedly than anything that comes thereafter. Conversely, given the tradition of cop shows being named for their leads and the fact that the series is built so closely around a single protagonist, we might read the title as a reference to Tennison; is she the 'prime suspect' in the drama that follows, the outsider under suspicion, an interloper upsetting the masculine order of the Met Police? However one understands the title and wherever the pitch for the series sprang from exactly, Granada's interest was piqued and La Plante now had to make the imagined project a reality.

17

Her first priority was to begin research and get access to a real senior female police officer. Since her earliest work La Plante has cultivated a reputation for a commitment to meticulous, authenticated research pursued among the people and places she writes about, however dark the subject matter. For *Prime Suspect 3*, for example, she immersed herself in central London's homeless and rent-boy communities, while her other research over the years has included interviews with some of Britain's most notorious murderers, including Myra Hindley, Peter Sutcliffe and Dennis Nilsen.[17] To prepare for *Prime Suspect* she contacted the Metropolitan Police and asked to meet a female officer working as 'a high-ranking detective in a homicide division'.[18] There were only a handful of potential candidates. But one of them, DCI Jackie Malton, met with La Plante and agreed to help her.

La Plante subsequently received unparalleled access to police work in her research alongside Malton, shadowing her in incident rooms and police labs over a number of months till she'd developed a sufficient grasp of forensics and police protocol to proceed. La Plante has consequently acknowledged a great debt to Malton for *Prime Suspect*'s success and for the invaluable knowledge she brought to the script. With Malton's help, and after some initial nervousness at Granada about how Tennison's aloofness would be received, *Prime Suspect* was finally put into production by executive producer Sally Head.

Meet 'The Real Jane Tennison'

The extraordinary reception of *Prime Suspect* led to a flurry of media interest in 'the real Jane Tennison'. In the coverage of Jackie Malton that followed, many of the experiences she described seemed familiar, having already been dramatised to memorable effect by La Plante. In a 1993 interview, Malton commented, 'The plot and the character were hers, but the authenticity was mine ... . I'd tell her something one day and the next day it'd be in the script'.[19] Appearing in the 1999 Channel 4 documentary series *Coppers* about the history of policing in the UK, Malton described how negotiating sexual harassment had been part of her everyday life in the force ('A Job for the Gentle Sex', tx 9/9/1999). As one of the few women ever to make it into the macho world of the elite Metropolitan Police Flying Squad, charged with overseeing serious crime such as armed robbery, she recalls 'In the police [women] were a bike or a dyke'. The early scene in *Prime Suspect* where Otley and Jones maliciously speculate about whether Tennison 'is one' or not (in Otley's charming words, 'Do me a favour, what man would want that?') might well have come directly from Malton's own memoirs. Indeed, just as Otley recurrently refers to Tennison as 'that tart', in the same episode of *Coppers* one of Malton's former Flying Squad colleagues blithely recalls how Malton's nickname there had been 'The Tart'.

18

'The authenticity was mine': former DCI Jackie Malton, the inspiration behind Tennison

In the same programme, though, Malton describes too how she also felt compelled to participate in this male culture in order to 'be accepted as one of them', joining the lads for their boozy curries and drinking sessions. 'I was a party to it ... but I wanted to stay', she comments, a sensibility evident in Tennison too given her regular invitations to colleagues to come for drinks after work. Interestingly, Malton also reveals just how beguiling she found the macho media representations of her department's work; real life and TV drama collapse into one another again as she tells how she used to hum the dramatic theme tune of the popular 1970s action-led Flying Squad cop show *The Sweeney* when she went out on a job, recalling 'And the fear and the adrenaline rush was just fantastic, it was huge ... . The Flying Squad for me was the ultimate'.

So often did Malton's name feature in articles about *Prime Suspect* and such was the interest generated in her that Malton went on to forge a media career of her own, making frequent appearances in media documentaries and newspaper articles. Sharing insights not just about *Prime Suspect* but about policing and her experience of being a female detective more widely, she later became an adviser to La Plante on the accuracy of police protocol in her scripts. Recognising a niche in the media marketplace arising from the growth of crime drama since the 1990s, on leaving the Met Police Malton set up her own company, 'Prime Crime', specialising in advising film and TV makers on police storylines. As her website announces (www.primecrime.com) the company, 'assists writers in state of the art police procedures, story texture, story ideas and characters ... [Malton] has nearly 30 years service with the Metropolitan Police Force'. Yet Prime Crime also underlines Malton's credentials to potential clients by pointing to her relationship with her *fictional* counterpart, with the company website itself calling Malton 'the real Detective Chief Inspector Jane Tennison'. Presented in this manner, it is almost as if this claim to fame makes her a *bona fide* expert in a way her police CV alone would not.

Cops on the Box: Television's '*Terra Firma*'

What all this points to is how the evolution of *Prime Suspect* needs to be understood not only within the context of a network of individual writers, producers and consultants, but also within particular generic and institutional histories. In particular, the entwining of police and media interests in the Malton/*Prime Suspect* narrative described above says much about the interdependent relations between the two institutions. Malton's evident professional and personal investment in the making of *Prime Suspect* underlines the significance of the tangled relationship between 'realism', TV crime drama and actual police work. In relation to this, Charlotte Brunsdon has argued that the genre maintains a heightened 'reality effect'.[20] She suggests it operates an 'internal realism' built upon its intertextuality and continued use of particular codes and conventions, so that its sense of realism ultimately 'has more to do with the reality constructed in other crime series than with reality as such "out there" '.[21] Cop and crime shows have undeniably enjoyed a rich and extensive history in popular television since the medium's early years, both in the UK and US. In the US, one of

20

the first, highly pivotal long-running TV series was police detective drama *Dragnet* (NBC, 1951–9), a show which prided itself on its attention to the everyday detail of work in the LAPD, aspiring to quasi-documentary credentials by using real police jargon and researching genuine cases for material. In the UK, *Dixon of Dock Green* had one of the longest series runs in British television history, having been on air on the BBC from 1955 to 1976. Almost two decades after its demise, in 1994 Ellis Cashmore observed that crime drama 'regularly occupies 20 per cent of program time',[22] a figure which has surely been exceeded again in the 2000s given the success of *CSI: Crime Scene Investigation* and its associated spin-offs and imitators. As Cashmore has argued, the genre 'beats that of soaps in terms of longevity. While moods and tastes have shifted over the decades, crime drama has been television's *terra firma*'.[23]

Given the long prominence of crime series on television it is important to situate *Prime Suspect* within the broader history of the cop show, both to demonstrate how it is inevitably embedded in this history and how it moved on from it. One of the key debates that scholars and critics have tussled with in order to account for the enduring popularity of the cop-show format has been the extent to which it fulfils a (conservative) function in wider culture and society as 'a genre of reassurance'. Throughout their history, and despite superficial changes of inflection, in many instances police dramas have essentially represented the police as the determined protectors of society, concerned guardians who ensure that villains are justly locked away. At the same time, as the genre developed some series posed a challenge to this parochial view of caring cops. The BBC's *Law and Order* in 1978 was an early and controversial case in point, representing the police as not merely fallible but corrupt. In fact it can be argued that rather than serving only to endorse the status quo, the TV cop show is particularly well positioned to place difficult questions and social issues on television's agenda, and that *Prime Suspect* endeavoured to do precisely this.

In 1992, for example, *Prime Suspect 2* confronted the thorny subject of police racism head-on. This was an issue that had been troubling UK forces for years after a series of high-profile controversial

21

cases involving black communities, including the Brixton riots of 1981 and 1985, and widespread allegations of police violence towards black suspects and victims. From its opening scenes *Prime Suspect 2* plays with and foregrounds the police's (and even perhaps much of the general audience's) uncomfortable relationship with young black men. Tennison sits in an interview room quizzing a rape suspect who speaks with a thick Jamaican accent and arrogantly dismisses her questions, even making menacing intimations to her about white women liking it 'rough'. As her line of questioning becomes more insistent he starts to become angry, but just as their confrontation seems set to explode it is revealed that the whole scene is a role-play being filmed on video. The young black man is in fact a fellow police officer, DS Bob Oswalde (Colin Salmon) playing the part of a rape suspect on a police training exercise with Tennison. The scene is a provocative one for the manner in which it stirs the audience to reflect on their presumptions and

'Suspect' Robert Oswalde stares defiantly at Tennison in interview, before he is revealed to be a fellow detective

(mis-)reading of the exchange. It is able to turn the tables on the viewer precisely because it is evidently a novelty for a young black man to be a detective in a culture where minority groups are so poorly represented. (Later in *Prime Suspect 5* Tennison unwittingly discloses how she too is party to this prejudice when she attempts to move on a black bystander at a murder scene, only to learn he is DC Henry Adeliyeka (John Brobbey), a detective on her new Manchester team). As *Prime Suspect 2* continues, the marginalisation and prejudice suffered by Oswalde in the workplace come to parallel that endured by Tennison in the first series. 'I'm the same as you' he even tells her when she comments on how driven he is, a point underlined by the fact that they have a brief affair when they first meet.

But when an embarrassed Tennison subsequently finds herself having to work with Oswalde, she herself participates in his ostracism, undermining his place in the team by giving him junior tasks. Reprising the two-pronged, interlinked narrative structure of the first series, Oswalde's storyline is twinned with a crime plot in which Tennison's squad investigates the discovery of the buried remains of a young mixed-race girl. These two threads are entwined right from the start, when Oswalde's 'interview' is cut alongside chaotic scenes of the body being exhumed by forensic officers. The case is especially fraught since it takes place within a largely black London community where relations with police are highly volatile, following allegations that a local black boy charged with murdering a white youth had been 'fitted up'. Tennison argues that Oswalde's deployment onto 'Operation Nadine' will look tokenistic, a desperate effort by the Met to prove it isn't racist, but her resistance to his arrival is personal as much as professional. Anti-police feeling is stoked further still when black suspect Tony Allen (Fraser James), who had lived next door to the murder scene, is arrested by Oswalde and dies in police custody. No-one is brought to account for his death, with Thorndike's internal investigation resulting only in disciplinary papers being served on a handful of officers. This 'cover-up', along with scenes of disillusioned locals criticising PR-driven 'community policing' meetings and Detective Inspector Burkin's (Craig

23

Fairbrass) unabashed racism, echoed suspicions about police behaviour being debated widely across the UK. The programme even alludes to similar conflict in the real world of policing when Tennison encourages Oswalde to see a psychologist as he struggles to cope with Tony's death, telling him 'It's a friend of mine. She helped someone who was at Broadwater Farm. She's good'.[24] *Prime Suspect* thus sits uneasily within the 'genre of reassurance' model. While there is no question that Tennison is wholly dedicated to her work she is also seen to be highly fallible, working within a system evidently riddled with corruption and egotism.

Critics have also charted how shifts in crime drama might be understood as responses to the changing status of the police and attitudes to crime in 'the real world'. Such work has helped entrench a canon of landmark series in British crime drama history, some of which it will be helpful to explore briefly here by way of indicating the pedigree that preceded *Prime Suspect*.[25] Scholar Robert Reiner has argued that 'the changing image of the TV cop' can be traced through the shifting balance of representation between that of 'carers' and 'controllers'.[26] He suggests that historically, an image of the police as carers was expressly cultivated in Britain when the police force was established, intended to head off resistance from pro-libertarians. By the middle of the twentieth century, in a 'post-World War II climate of social and political consensus',[27] it appeared that this tactic had been successful given the prevalence of an idealised image of the community 'bobby-on-the-beat'. It was within such a climate that a series like *Dixon of Dock Green* could flourish, depicting a world in which the ordinary British copper's lot still consisted largely of dealing with relatively harmless incidental crime and being out on the beat on his 'patch'. For Dixon, policing the community meant being *part* of the community and he dealt overwhelmingly with the everyday – a spate of bicycle thefts ('Crawford's First Pinch') or a break-in at the local pinball palace ('Little Boy Blue') – rather than the remarkable. The serious crimes and constant internal wrangling at the centre of each *Prime Suspect* underline how such a vision of localised policing now seems to have been consigned to history. But Tennison reveals a tentative nostalgia for it in *Prime Suspect 5* when she has to give a presentation to a group of disaffected inner-city schoolkids. 'People are always saying that the police should liaise with the community. But I believe they should be a part of the community', she tells her teenage audience. Tellingly, their less-than-enthusiastic response suggests that they remain unconvinced by her hesitant words and unmoved by the institution of the police.

Such disillusionment with policing can be traced back over some years in the UK. Social and industrial shifts during *Dixon*'s run, including rising unemployment and a spate of strikes (later corresponding with the advent of Thatcherism), meant that by the 1970s British culture was understood as increasingly marked by dissent and division. Within this climate public support for the police also declined. While its routine focus on an affable uniformed London copper had initially been lauded for its realism, *Dixon* now appeared an implausible and anachronistic figure. In order to keep in step with changes in society, television required fresh police protagonists and a revised perspective on policing. *Z Cars* (BBC, 1962–78), with its group of flawed but dedicated cops hand-picked to form a new mobile police division, can be seen as a transitional series in this shift. But the representative British show typically invoked as the apex of this transformation is *The Sweeney*. Enjoying huge success in the 1970s, it established another cultural icon in its tough-guy, maverick protagonist, DI Jack Regan (John Thaw). Uniformed officers or 'plods' were traded for plain-clothes detectives in the Met Police's elite Flying Squad ('Sweeney Todd' being the unit's moniker in cockney rhyming slang). The circles Regan moved in could not have been more removed from Dixon's, often requiring him to be every bit as brash and violent as the criminals he was up against.

The Sweeney is still widely and even affectionately remembered in British popular culture for its macho posturing, car chases, squealing tyres and frequent fisticuffs. Most recently its conventions have been parodied and interrogated by the BBC's playful period crime series, *Life on Mars* (2006–7), with its thuggish but

25

dedicated anti-hero DCI Gene Hunt (Philip Glenister). In its day, though, *The Sweeney* had brought new levels of violence to the cop show just as Britain moved into an era of so-called 'law-and-order' politics. It is precisely this overtly white, masculine era and style of policing that DCI John Shefford embodies at the start of the investigation in the first *Prime Suspect* and which the series implicitly suggests must be tempered with greater accountability and diversity. With his loud, coarse manner and fixation on charging Marlow in record time rather than being attentive to the evidence ('We're going to break Paxman's record, go, go go!') Shefford pays the price for adopting the combative approach of *Sweeney*-style policing, when he dies of a heart attack halfway through a meeting in Superintendent Kernan's office.

It is impossible not to be curious about how changes or periods of crises in real policing might be engaged with or contained by their fictional TV counterparts. But such a 'reflectionist' approach risks

26

The demise of an old-school cop: Shefford collapses and dies at the station

neglecting other factors such as industrial and technological determinants which also need to be considered in periods of shifting representation. Dixon had come to appear dated not merely at an ideological level but in its slow-paced aesthetics, as British audiences enjoyed increasing access to more spectacular action-based American TV imports such as *Kojak* (CBS, 1973–8), and vigilante cop movies like *Dirty Harry* (Don Siegel, 1971). The introduction of newly inflected shows like *The Sweeney* therefore needs to be understood also in terms of the *business* of television and the necessity for generic reinvention, as much as in external factors like the state of British politics and the rise of law-and-order campaigning.

The 1980s proved a highly fraught period for the British police, with a series of urban riots in the early 1980s and violent clashes with striking miners during the miners' strike of 1984–5. Interestingly in relation to the idea that the genre stands as a mirror to real-life shifts in policing, television cop shows of the period did not tend to reflect the level of anti-police sentiment circulating at this time, with successful series such as *The Gentle Touch* and *Juliet Bravo* (BBC, 1980–5) centring on honest and dedicated officers. These programmes might well be seen as serving to rehabilitate the image of the police during a period of crisis for the institution. Reiner's 'carers vs controllers' approach to the cop series provides some useful language with which to examine it. But the overly simplistic nature of such a dichotomy becomes apparent when faced with the ambivalent outlook on policing palpable in a series like *Prime Suspect*. Even while Tennison is figured as an ardent 'carer', much of the institution of the police is figured as '*out of* control' (and beyond hers) with some officers writing their own rules at times. While making an arrest in *Prime Suspect 4: The Lost Child*, for example, DI Muddyman (Jack Ellis) viciously attacks an (allegedly rehabilitated) paedophile who has become the prime suspect in the kidnap and murder of a baby girl. There is no question that this officer is a loose cannon who has crossed a line, even though the programme sympathetically suggests that his aggression is prompted by Muddyman's having himself been the victim of child

27

abuse. When Muddyman jeopardises the inquiry and flouts police ethics by showing the suspect's girlfriend confidential video footage of her boyfriend undergoing therapy, Tennison takes him to task privately, but it remains unclear what happens to Muddyman as a result. The programme evades a resolution to this plot thread since the police hearing into the case takes place behind closed doors and the audience is never privy to what Tennison reveals – or conceals – there.

Brunsdon has observed that as it moved into the late 1980s and early 1990s, a 'structure of anxiety' became apparent in British crime drama. In her words, the genre 'in this period speaks very directly to the concerns of a Great Britain in decline under a radical Conservative government with a strong rhetoric of law and order', with the police series becoming 'a privileged site for the staging of the trauma of the breakup of the postwar settlement'.[28] Numerous commentators have noted like Brunsdon that crime drama proliferated and diversified in Britain during this period, but for Brunsdon, all TV crime fiction of this period was affected by discourses of Equal Opportunities. This was nowhere clearer than in *Prime Suspect*, in which the 'structure of anxiety' is explicitly embodied by the presence of a woman and social discord is signalled when for the first time *a female officer* is promoted to lead a murder inquiry. In the next chapter, I look at some of the history of women in TV crime drama and how *Prime Suspect* shook this history up, asking not only what happens to the cop show when a woman takes the lead; but what happens to women when they take the lead in a cop show?

2 It's a Fair Cop: Women and TV Crime Drama

When one reflects on the best-known and best-loved detectives within TV crime drama and beyond, the extent to which male names loom large in this 'men's genre'[29] soon becomes apparent. Sherlock Holmes and Poirot; Kojak and Starsky and Hutch; Morse and Frost; Philip Marlowe, Dirty Harry *et al.*; the list is a lengthy one. Yet despite the prominence of these and other male protagonists throughout the history of crime fiction, a number of the finer attributes we might admire or expect to find in a good detective are generally thought of in wider cultural terms as 'female'. An attention to detail; the capacity to listen and 'read' people; the ability to multitask as clues and leads mount; all of these characteristics are typically (though not unproblematically) culturally designated 'feminine'. The brash, action-led vision of policing seen in cop dramas from *The Sweeney* to *The Shield* (FX, 2002–8) constitutes only one model of detective work – one overtly masculine strand within the history of the genre. Another more meditative approach, represented by figures such as Columbo and Inspector Morse, has an equally prevalent history where detective skills are not played out within the context of a tough masculinity at all. In this chapter I examine how gender has been pivotal to the frameworks of the TV cop show before exploring how Tennison expanded the dramatic terrain of the female cop. Looking at some of the history of women and policing, both in 'the real world' and on the small screen, I examine how *Prime Suspect* proved to be so innovative and controversial in its exploration of this theme.

An Unsuitable Job for a Woman?

The notions of logic and emotion are crucial to debates about the gendering of detection. Within gendered binary oppositions, 'logic', a capacity for rational thought, is seen as a 'male' attribute and lies in opposition to 'female' emotiveness. In the first *Prime Suspect* Tennison mocks the great tradition of 'male' ratiocinative detection; noting that Peter's ex-wife is only letting their son Joey (Jeremy Warder) visit him more often because she's pregnant, she then taps herself on the forehead and exclaims ironically 'See? Sherlock Holmes!' It was women's presumed physical frailty and emotional vulnerability that for so long meant they were excluded from serving in the police, and remained largely absent in the canon of classic fictional detectives. But turning the gendering of detective work on its head again for a moment, what exactly is meant by 'having a hunch', that elusive, non-corroborative but invariably vindicated gut feeling that has guided so many of the great detectives? Surely it is nothing more than the male equivalent of good old-fashioned 'feminine instinct'? Tennison herself situates her *modus operandi* within this school, telling DI Clare Devanney (Julia Lane) in *Prime Suspect 5* 'I only know one way to work and that's through instinct, instinct and slog'. Similarly, the much-derided 'feminine' attribute of 'nosiness' becomes a desirable (male) trait in the figure of the detective when it is repositioned instead as 'an enquiring mind'. It is interesting to note in this regard that the most famous female detective of all, Agatha Christie's Miss Marple, is figured not as an incisive intellect but as a slightly dotty, inquisitive old lady.

Despite the fact that many traditionally 'female' skills might be thought of as excellent foundations for a good detective, for many years women were excluded from the police force both in the US and UK. In this respect their relative absence in early TV crime drama mirrors their real-life exclusion from police work. In the UK, women were finally admitted into the police during World War I, following a campaign by women suffragists who complained about their treatment at the hands of an all-male police force. Their conditions in the years that followed were, however, rather different to men's. Working for less money, albeit in return for fewer and less antisocial hours, they dealt with women and children rather than 'serious' crime. Like other regional forces, London's Metropolitan Police had a separate 'Women's Police Department' but by 1973, in response to the growing pressure of the women's movement and in advance of the Sex Discrimination Act requiring it by law, this had been integrated so that men and women now worked alongside one another. Nevertheless, early in *Prime Suspect* we see how some of the gendered distinctions regarding police work have proved resilient. When Tennison complains to Kernan that she's tired of doing paperwork while waiting to lead a murder investigation, she notes that she spent five years at Reading having to oversee 'sex cases'. Nominally the pathway to equal opportunities and seniority had been opened up to women officers. But in reality it remained very much a job for the boys, as the dismally small number of women DCIs in the Met Police available to assist La Plante in her research for *Prime Suspect* underlined.

Despite the long exclusion of women from real-life policing and the proliferation of male protagonists throughout the history of crime fiction, female detectives have a history in literature and (to a lesser extent) cinema predating television. From the Nancy Drew mysteries, to Dorothy Sayers's Harriet Vane novels, to Nora Charles in *The Thin Man* movie series of the 1930s–40s, this history suggests that a taste for female sleuths has long been present. Furthermore, though TV cop shows were once peopled overwhelmingly by male police, we should be wary of presuming that these series only began to win over women audiences when they began to adopt female stars. The female audience for TV crime remains largely unknown, having been subject to

31

very little critical enquiry. In contrast it is widely agreed that literary detective fiction, along with true-crime writing, has traditionally attracted large and loyal female readerships. Over the last three decades particularly, a number of women writers with women detective protagonists have entered the ranks of crime literature's most successful and prolific authors. Linda Mizejewski suggests that 'fans claim the turning point was 1982, when Sue Grafton and Sara Paretsky introduced their female P.I. series',[30] featuring Kinsey Millhone and V. I. Warshawski. Then in 1990, shortly before *Prime Suspect* appeared, Patricia Cornwell published *Postmortem*, the first of the best-selling Dr Kay Scarpetta novels narrated by the sleuthing forty-something forensics medical examiner. Real-life forensic anthropologist Kathy Reichs's highly successful series about forensic anthropologist Temperance Brennan débuted in 1997 with *Déjà Dead,* later inspiring the Fox series *Bones*. Both of these women authors and their heroines can be seen as prime movers in the cultural turn towards a fascination with forensics evident since the early 1990s.

32 These book series are also part of a cultural shift which has seen the gradual ascendancy of the female detective across popular culture. In this respect, 1991 proved to be a signal year not only marking the broadcast of *Prime Suspect*, but the enormous critical and popular success of *The Silence of the Lambs* (Jonathan Demme), starring Jodie Foster in an Oscar-winning performance as FBI agent Clarice Starling. Like Tennison, Starling embarks on a testing quest to track down a brutal misogynistic serial killer, a journey in which her own femininity and isolation in a male-dominated world forms part of the drama's investigative drive. Though they premièred just weeks apart, the film and series feature a strikingly analogous early scene which underlines their shared outlook. Both Starling and Tennison are shown diminutively framed in a workplace elevator filled with male colleagues who dwarf them with their bulk and masculine presence, accentuating their difference and segregation as women. When Shefford and his team pile through the doors at the start of the Marlow case, chatting among themselves and ignoring Tennison, she is squeezed to the back and her

ostracism becomes visual as well as symbolic. Both women also demonstrate a perceptive 'feminine' attention to the clues left behind by the dead women's bodies, with Tennison noting that Karen Howard is unlikely to have been a prostitute because of her 'expensive boutique-type' clothes, while Starling observes one victim is from town because of her 'glitter nail polish'.[31] But even prior to this landmark year, it had become evident early in the 1980s that a shift was underway both in crime literature and the television police series as a number of new shows centring on women protagonists emerged, including *Cagney & Lacey* (CBS, 1982–8) in the US and *The Gentle Touch* (1980–4) and *Juliet Bravo* (1980–5) in the UK.

In an institutional sense, this new 'twist' within crime drama can be seen as a further instance of the cop show simply renewing itself and bringing new inflections to bear in order to avoid becoming stale. At the same time, these series seemed to be responding to real-life social

33

Squeezed out, in every sense: Tennison shares an elevator with Shefford and co. ...

... while Clarice Starling is similarly dwarfed by her male colleagues in *The Silence of the Lambs*

changes as women gradually became more visible in the police and other 'masculine' and high-profile professions (including a female Prime Minister, Margaret Thatcher, coming to power in the UK in 1979). But beyond this too, these new series were a means for TV crime drama to work through emergent cultural trends and anxieties during what Mizejewski has called a 'law-and-order revival'. She notes that this was precipitated in the US by the disquieting endings of both the Vietnam War and the Nixon presidency, suggesting that the era's new network shows about women cops were a response to a period of troubling change.[32] Alongside these, a whole new slew of sympathetic male cops including *Starsky and Hutch* (ABC, 1975–9) and *Kojak* appeared. These figures 'infused the networks' with a series of tough guys who were also 'decent, fair, vulnerable human beings', presenting a vision of police integrity in stark contrast to contemporary US news images of police as 'helmeted riot forces'.[33]

Examining the British context, Gillian Dyer has argued that the comforting image of local, benevolent policing offered by *Juliet Bravo* fulfilled a kind of positive police PR function at a time when their work was being increasingly scrutinised. The series centred on Inspector

34

Jean Darblay (Stephanie Turner, later replaced by Anna Carteret as Inspector Kate Longton) as the boss of a police station in Hartley, a fictional working-class northern town. Dyer suggests that *Juliet Bravo*

> was introduced at a time when women's liberation had become a safe media topic and when the image of policing was in need of reassessment … [it] worked to portray the police in compassionate and caring terms at a time when there was some cynicism about police methods in the wider society.[34]

For many, this growing discontentment with aggressive policing was borne out in spectacular fashion shortly after the arrival of *The Gentle Touch* and *Juliet Bravo*, when nearly 300 police officers were injured during three days of anti-police riots in Brixton in April 1981. The violence followed the arrest of a man under a controversial (and allegedly racist) stop-and-search policy. Similar protests were repeated

35

Stephanie Turner as Inspector Jean Darblay, the first star of *Juliet Bravo*

just three months later during rioting in Liverpool.[35] These heated, anxious, urban environments were quite a contrast with the world of Inspector Jean Darblay. Even though Hartley is far from a rural idyll, it is nevertheless a place where Jean's small team of officers generally knows the locals and where the police appear to be accessible to the community. The series quickly established that Jean's fight against the chauvinism of an all-male team would be an ongoing theme; 'Don't ever open a car door for me or an office door, I can do that for myself!' she tells one of them early on, a sentiment that could have come straight from Jane Tennison. Nevertheless, by episode two Darblay is supplying tea and womanly sympathy at the station to kindly, elderly embezzler Doris, to the extent that she even visits Doris's house to feed her cat for her while she's locked up. It's difficult to imagine that Kojak would have done the same.

The Gentle Touch, starring Jill Gascoigne as Detective Inspector Maggie Forbes, had premièred some four months prior to Juliet Bravo, in April 1980. The series initially seemed to promise a grittier look at a senior police woman's working life, with Forbes working as a plain-clothes detective and not a uniformed officer. Set in London rather than rural Lancashire, the opening credits primed the audience for a tough drama, featuring a startling montage of grainy black-and-white reportage-style images of bullet-holes in glass, street protests and police under siege. The first episode established that, like Jean Darblay, Maggie is the main breadwinner in her household since she is married to another officer considerably junior in rank. But we quickly learn that her husband Ray is troubled and severely disillusioned by police work. The episode sympathetically shows the flipside of the era's anti-police feeling from a police perspective, as Ray tells Maggie he is tired of being publicly abused and plans to resign. Lamenting the demise of the 'bobby-on-the-beat' he declares 'We aren't coppers any more are we Maggie, or bobbies ... we're the fuzz, the filth, pigs ... they're always on about *their* rights but what about *our* rights? ... I'm leaving the force, I mean it.' Tragically he never gets the chance, since later that day Ray is shot and killed as he heroically intervenes in an

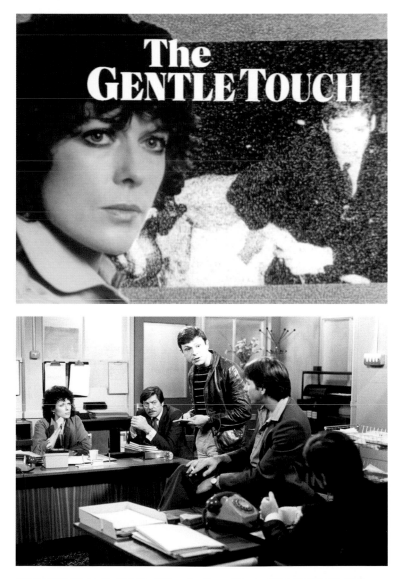

Jill Gascoigne as DI Maggie Forbes in the gritty opening credits to *The Gentle Touch* and at work surrounded by male colleagues

armed robbery while off duty. Though placing Maggie in a senior police role, charged with some challenging cases and having to prove herself as a woman working in a male environment, the programme always weighed Maggie's professional life against a vision of her in a *domestic* life; mother to a teenage son, daughter to a loving father, and as played by the strikingly attractive Jill Gascoigne, her femininity was never in question. In the light of such series, Dyer warns against presuming that merely introducing female protagonists into the cop show could inherently change these programmes in any significant way. Such roles in themselves '[do] not question the aesthetics and conventions of the male crime series through which meanings are in part realised' she concluded, arguing that *Juliet Bravo* in particular 'leaves undisturbed the framework of male police structures of the crime series and does not enable the questioning of women's relationship to the law and consensus morality'.[36]

New York's Finest

More interesting in this respect was the landmark American series *Cagney & Lacey*. The series' innovation was not so much to make a show featuring a female police detective *per se*. Rather it was to develop a duo of committed close-knit women cops, working as partners and looking out for each other on the streets of New York. In fact, as Julie D'Acci has documented, the programme was explicitly conceived as a response to a prominent book from the women's movement, Molly Haskell's *From Reverence to Rape: The Treatment of Women in the Movies* (1974). After series' writers Barbara Avedon and Barbara Corday read Haskell's feminist film history they were struck by the realisation that there had never been the equivalent of a female 'buddy movie'.[37] With this premise in mind, quite unlike the bulk of crime drama in TV history *Cagney & Lacey* was very consciously targeted and constructed as a 'woman's programme'. The protagonists were both colleagues and friends, and spoke to different kinds of women's interests since one of them was a married mother (Lacey) and the other a more single-minded career officer (Cagney).

The series had originally been developed as a film, but clashes had emerged between the writers and producer Barney Rosenzweig and the studios over issues including the protagonists' alleged lack of 'femininity'. A potential MGM deal stalled over their insistence on securing well-known 'sex-symbol' actresses for the leads. As a result the project languished for years before being resurrected for television. D'Acci provides a fascinating case study of the tribulations the show went through before eventually securing its place as a weekly series. Its initial outing as a widely publicised CBS made-for-TV-movie in 1981 was trailed with high-profile feminist endorsement from the likes of Gloria Steinem. Starring established TV 'sex-siren' actress Loretta Swit from *M*A*S*H* (CBS, 1972–83) as Cagney, with Tyne Daly as Lacey, it won such impressive audience figures that CBS committed to a regular series. With Meg Foster replacing Swit due to her *M*A*S*H* commitments, initial series rating were poor, however, and the show was very nearly cancelled. Rescheduling improved audience figures but a press and industry debate was soon underway regarding whether the two women were too tough and 'women's lib'. There was speculation that audiences would perceive them as 'dykes' and switch off and, in particular, that the unmarried and therefore more threatening Cagney as played by Foster was insufficiently feminine. In response her character was given a more respectable upper-middle-class background and a revamped wardrobe, and Foster was replaced by Sharon Gless (who, rather ironically given CBS's nervousness about Foster's image, soon established a large lesbian fan-base). Employing significant numbers of women as writers, producers, creative consultants and story editors, *Cagney & Lacey* would go on to amass numerous awards. Applauded for its willingness to tackle topics such as 'single, working mothers, federal cutbacks in social services programmes, nuclear irresponsibility and inhuman treatment of "illegal aliens", as well as race, class and gender',[38] it became known as one of the most politically conscious, liberally minded programmes on television.

Cagney & Lacey was embraced by audiences for its female heroines and politically conscious storylines

The programme's troubled production history, and the programme-makers' efforts to contain the character of Cagney in particular, demonstrate how the figure of the woman cop and the question of her femininity was and remains problematic for television. The programme empathetically tackled women's anxieties about the conflict between career and family by contrasting two professional women protagonists, one of whom had a husband and children and one of whom did not. But the programme's preoccupation with the issues arising from this, and the focus on Cagney and Lacey as women friends as much as women cops, came to be perceived by some commentators as its eventual weakness. With its attention to the women's personal lives over and above 'action', the programme was accused of having diluted its cop-show credentials, with plotlines including Lacey's breast cancer and Cagney's pregnancy scare. Furthermore, in their work with the vulnerable and disenfranchised the women seemed sometimes to take on the function of social workers rather than NYPD detectives, so that while it was unquestionably a milestone for the representation of women on television, for many the show eventually came to resemble soap opera more than cop drama. Was this the fate that would inevitably ensue when women entered TV crime drama?

'She's not what I expected'

This was the context of TV's women cops into which Jane Tennison appeared and in which she was widely heralded as the most nuanced and intelligent depiction of a police woman yet seen on the small screen. What made *Prime Suspect* so compelling for these first audiences was the series' deft balancing act, exploring Tennison as subject to a breadth of emotions on the one hand and maintaining the intrigue and detail of a police procedural on the other. It is telling that when Peter's ex-wife Marianne (Francesca Ryan) meets Tennison for the first time at home she remarks that 'She's not what I expected. I don't know, I suppose I thought she'd be in uniform'. Tennison later quips that she 'should've worn a flat hat for her', but it is more than the lack of police dress which throws Marianne off-guard. What exactly *was* she expecting? Tennison's appearance in this scene is certainly rendered feminine; warmly lit by the softer tones that distinguish this domestic space from the office and incident room, she wears an elegant pencil skirt with a flattering cream silk blouse and simple gold jewellery, an outfit quite removed from the sombre attire of police uniform. In a rare comic moment, she has accidentally covered the blouse in the chocolate cake she bought to welcome Peter's young son Joey (Jeremy Warder). This human touch, and the maternal ease with which she quickly befriends Joey and takes his hand, derail Marianne's assumptions about Tennison's 'toughness'. Throughout all the series, in fact, there are intermittent private glimpses of Tennison reapplying her make-up or

41

A woman's touch: Tennison reapplies her make-up before entering the taped-interview room

arranging her hair, moments which suggest her awareness of the importance of her outward femininity. Interestingly, a number of these moments come just before she interviews a witness or suspect, as if a fresh coat of lipstick is part of the armour she brings with her in preparation for these potentially volatile encounters.

In fact, Tennison consistently plays out 'unexpected' qualities and interweaves both 'masculine' and 'feminine' traits. While the series is careful to trace moments underlining her femininity, Tennison also displays certain stereotypically male attributes – punching the air when she gets a result, smoking and drinking with relish, wanting to be known as 'guv'nor or boss'. She can seem to savour the simultaneous prestige and strife wrought by police work; outside the incident room after she has given her first briefing to the team, the look of relief and satisfaction on her face as she closes her eyes and lights up a cigarette is almost sexual. Furthermore, despite her own experiences as a woman fighting to secure her place in a profession populated by chauvinist bullies, she evidently does not feel it is incumbent on her to help ease the path of other women coming up through the ranks. As she puts it bluntly to woman DS Chris Cromwell (Sophie Stanton) in *Prime Suspect 4: Inner Circles*, 'If you're looking for any favours, you're looking in the wrong place. Understand?' In the first *Prime Suspect* she gives little recognition to Woman Police Constable Maureen Havers's (Mossie Smith) contribution, after Havers provides the lead that links the women to Marlow by observing that the victims had manicured nails and Moyra had been a beautician. After finally securing Marlow's confession Tennison stops Havers in the corridor, not to enjoy a little female camaraderie but only to enquire 'Any of those lads about?' Later, in *Prime Suspect 5*, Tennison actually goes out of her way to exclude DI Clare Devanney from the inner circle of her murder investigation, seemingly threatened by this young 'fast-tracked' achiever, in whom she

Tennison enjoys a cigarette after facing off with Otley and delivering her first briefing to the team

perhaps sees echoes of herself. And in *Prime Suspect 6* she shows scant regard for Equal Opportunities legislation when she asks Detective Lorna Greaves (Tanya Moodie) whether she is really cut out to be on a murder squad, given that, as the mother of two young children, she can't hope to put in the necessary extra hours.

Conscientious and tenacious, Tennison is also flawed (her very name evokes the word 'tension'), with her on-off battle to quit smoking becoming symbolic of her fallibility. She can be contradictory too; while she outwardly condemns the force's propensity for cover-ups, for example, she colludes with Kernan to keep quiet about Otley's evidence-tampering in exchange for choosing his replacement. She can also be selfish and aloof at times, as seen in her unfeeling and persistent handling of Karen Howard's clearly distraught boyfriend and father in her first murder case. When the evidently conservative Major Howard (Michael Fleming) firmly insists he wants to speak to a male officer about his daughter's murder, Tennison thoughtlessly starts to argue the point with him till Burkin has to take her outside and tell her, 'Leave him alone! Jesus Christ, let the man cry, he's heartbroken!' But Tennison quickly understands how tactlessly she has behaved. In a poignant moment, as both she and we are shut out from Howard's rush of grief behind the closed door, she pauses and moans out loud at the realisation, putting her head in her hands.

For as much as she can be austere and single-minded, Tennison can also be movingly empathetic and human. As the series progresses a succession of small moments intimate the sensitivity that lies beneath her often cool exterior. Significantly, these exchanges are sometimes figured by her willingness to *touch*. To offer comfort through touch is to cross a line as a police officer, since it breaches 'proper' distance and professionalism. It implies an empathy or emotionalism which is at odds with the rationalism so often revered in detective work. For, equally, the desire to offer comfort through touch is also understood as a particularly '*feminine*' response. In those moments when Tennison reaches out to a victim or suspect to console them the audience is reminded of her female difference, since it is difficult to imagine her

male counterparts doing the same. In *Prime Suspect 2*, for example, a
distressed Sarah Allen (Jenny Jules) finally confesses her 'awful secret' to
Tennison, admitting that she and her brother Tony had witnessed the
rape of Joanne Fagunwa (Nina Sosanya), the teenage girl murdered and
buried next door to them. Though Sarah has aggravated and challenged
Tennison throughout the case, Tennison's reaction is nevertheless to go
to her and put her arms around her as Sarah releases years of repressed
guilt and terror at last. Later, in *Prime Suspect 4: The Lost Child*, Susan
Covington (Beatie Edney), the distraught mother of a murdered baby,
startlingly confesses to Tennison that she killed the child herself. Driven
to distraction by the endless pressure of being a single working mother
caring for a demanding infant, she had finally cracked at her baby's
crying; 'She ... she took so much. Everything. She would not be satisfied,
would not let me sleep ...'. Tennison passes no judgement at this
revelation and betrays no anger at the wrongful arrest or hours of
wasted police work Covington's actions have precipitated. Instead as the
clearly traumatised woman begins to scream 'I'm sorry!' Tennison turns
to her, holds her, soothes her.   45

     The series' most interesting scene in this regard comes also in
Prime Suspect 2 as Tennison attends the hospital bedside of David
Harvey (Tom Watson). The former tenant of the house where Joanne
Fagunwa's remains were found, he is Tennison's prime suspect and now
terminally ill. In his dimly lit room, he lies in a pool of light as she sits
beside him in shadow, waiting for him to talk and acutely aware that
this may be her last opportunity to secure a confession. In an effort to
win him round she tells him she's Catholic too ('It's been a long time
since my last confession') and encourages him to release himself from
the burden of the crime; 'I remember [that] feeling of relief, you know?
A great weight being lifted off your shoulders ... . You're dying David.
Why don't you just get it off your chest ... you can talk to me'. Through
all this she tends to him, speaking softly, evenly, calmly, giving him water
and holding his hand, not flinching from offering the comfort of her
touch even when he describes how he raped Joanne and how she
vomited when he gagged her. As their clasped hands lie at the

46

Tennison consoles Sarah Allen after she confesses her 'awful secret' in *Prime Suspect 2* and soothes a hysterical Susan Covington in *The Lost Child*

foreground of the image, centred in the light that falls on Harvey's bed, the presence of her touch is accentuated as she rhythmically strokes his hand.

It is a deeply disturbing scene at numerous levels. The horrific details contained in Harvey's confession (later proved false) make Tennison's willingness to comfort him seem grossly misplaced, though evidently effective in securing his declaration of guilt. The quietness of this carefully observed deathbed scene, punctuated by the steady beep of Harvey's heart monitor, is all the more affecting for the manner in which it is intercut with Oswalde's heavy-handed attempts to secure Tony's confession back at the station. Exhibiting an acute insensitivity, Oswalde hounds Tony relentlessly at his workplace and in the interview room. His barrage of angry questions and accusations continues even as it becomes increasingly clear that Tony is unstable and a danger to himself. As we cut back and forth between the hospital and station the techniques of each officer are vividly juxtaposed, with Tennison's calm, nurturing, reassuring (read 'feminine') approach contrasted powerfully with Oswalde's aggression and intimidation (read 'masculine'). But it later becomes apparent that Tennison has *played* femininity in this scene, exploiting her gender and employing the power of 'the gentle touch' to get results. Leaving Harvey's bedside she goes to the bathroom and washes her hands, wringing them out beneath a sign which cautions against the hot water in an effort to wash away her disgust, at Harvey and at her own insincerity. Looking at herself in the mirror, she pauses and studies her reflection for a moment, as if to reassure herself that she has not been permanently soiled by the pact she has made in that room.

In the first series, Tennison's ability to befriend the prostitutes in Oldham who knew one of the early victims, Jeannie, precipitates vital new evidence. Marginalised and belittled by the male officers who originally investigated the case, the women talk comfortably with Tennison in the pub over drinks, giving her a breakthrough lead on how the victims were 'strung up' which links the cases. Interestingly, too, as if to counter her own child-free status, throughout the series Tennison is

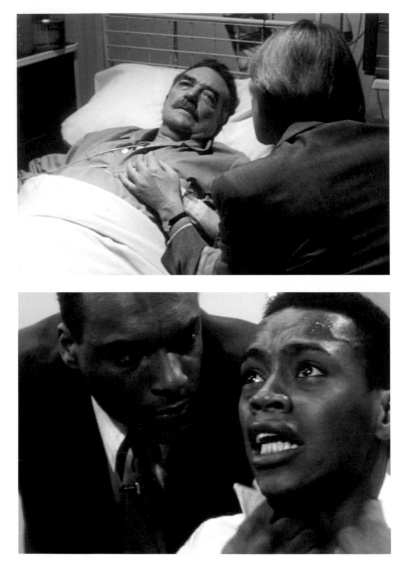

48

'You can talk to me': Tennison plays the femininity card with dying suspect David Harvey, while, in contrast, Oswalde aggressively bullies a distressed Tony Allen

shown to have a sensitive, reassuring way with children, a skill that more than once helps her on a case. Witness not only her bonding with Peter's son, but later the effortless way she chats in *Prime Suspect 6: The Last Witness* with Haweeya (Ann Warungu), the little girl living in the same overcrowded house as murdered Bosnian sisters Samira and Jasmina (Ingeborga Dapkunaite). After striking up a conversation with her in the communal hallway, Tennison learns details of a crucial phone call that Samira made which indicates she knew her killer. Later, in *Prime Suspect: The Final Act* Tennison persuades Destiny (Lakechia Jeanne), the terrified girl held hostage by her fugitive uncle, to hand over the gun she has just fired at him. Diffusing the situation by asking her amiably, 'You're not going to take that to school are you?', she then warmly takes the frightened child's hand and returns her safely to her mum.

In these moments *Prime Suspect* not only further humanises and feminises Tennison by endowing her with a (thwarted) maternal instinct, it obliquely suggests the uncompromising choices that her career has demanded of her as she foregoes any chance of a family life of her own for all-consuming dedication to the job. This is most explicitly dramatised in *Prime Suspect 3* when Tennison unexpectedly becomes pregnant and chooses to have a termination. As the series opens, Tennison has become involved with Jake Hunter (Michael J. Shannon), an American serial-killer expert visiting London on a book and lecture tour and a former lover of Tennison's still deeply smitten with her. As they temporarily rekindle their romance, we learn that years earlier he'd wanted them to marry and have children but she ended their relationship to concentrate on her career. History repeats itself as despite now being married with a family, Jake tries to persuade her again to come away with him. Tennison refuses, not least because she's about to start a new job at the Vice Squad. Their short-lived tryst is clumsily written and unconvincing, constituting one of the more hackneyed dramatic interludes of the series. Recalling La Plante's account of how she was pressurised by Granada to give more scope to Tennison's private life, one can almost sense her reluctance to write these scenes. As the

lovers say goodbye at the train station, Tennison hopes to get advice on
her latest case from Jake as well as to finish their relationship. She tells
him 'We're going to do exactly what we agreed to do. We're not going to
see each other again. You're going to get on that train and I'm going to
... Anyway, in the meantime ...'. 'I love you!' Jake interrupts. 'Yeah, I
know' she replies. 'So what's this case you're working on?' he continues
rather incongruously, as if remembering there's a police procedural to
get back to. The painfully awkward scene is proof evident that romantic
dialogue is not La Plante's forte.

But Tennison's subsequent pregnancy and eventual
termination do constitute another important facet of her personal
history, one which comes to inform how we read the scenes of her
befriending children and to wonder anew about her; does she ever regret
not having children of her own?; has her career been worth the life she
forewent? What is she thinking in *Prime Suspect 6* as she looks out at
Lorna Greaves from her office window, and watches her climb into her
car next to her husband as their children sleep peacefully in the back?
The series suggests motherhood could not be compatible with the kind
of professional life Tennison leads. It is significant that she arranges her
termination immediately after visiting Deputy Assistant Commissioner
Kennington's house during her investigation into a paedophile ring.
The child-abuse case which is the focus of *Prime Suspect 3* seems
deliberately juxtaposed with her own pregnancy, as if to instruct her of
the folly of having children in such a dark and sometimes hopeless
world. It is telling too that following her termination, the first part of
Prime Suspect 4 is called '*The Lost Child*' and sees Tennison
investigating the case of Susan Covington's murdered baby. The inquiry
constitutes one of the few cases where we actually see Tennison fight to
contain tears in front of others. In an attempt to fire up her team she tells
them about the tiny body of Vicky Warwick she's just seen lying in the
morgue and is momentarily overcome by emotion. When Covington
later admits to Tennison that she killed her own daughter, she is
accorded a lengthy confession in which she vividly debunks the myths of
conventional family life and motherhood:

The idea, the image that's shoved down your throat. It's a lie. You struggle to get a good job and then you struggle to keep it. You get a nice house and fill it with all the nice things you're supposed to fill it with and then you struggle to keep that. And you finish it off with a child … . Why should I suffer for what she did to me? I'm the victim. Suffocated since the beginning.

As Tennison comforts her and listens with evident sympathy, it is almost as if her own decision *not* to have a child is being vindicated by the case. Susan's postnatal breakdown serves to demonstrate both how motherhood can fail to deliver the fulfilment it promises and how social pressures on women mask the fact that motherhood is not the 'right' choice, not an innate given, for all women.

The Female Detective and (Not) 'Having It All'

Looked at another way though, the dilemmas Tennison faces about whether or how to try and have a relationship or family while in her profession are ones which have always existed for the figure of the dedicated, maverick cop. In the first *Prime Suspect*, as the case against Marlow mounts and progressively consumes Tennison, she inevitably begins to neglect Peter, who complains to her, 'The phone rings, I don't exist'. Equally, he seems perturbed by the compulsive streak in her which he is evidently seeing for the first time. 'Can I ask you something? Do you ever get emotionally involved? … . What about when you see them in the morgue?' he asks apprehensively one evening. His questions come after she has missed her elderly father's birthday party to make an appeal on '*Crime Night*'. Arriving late she then insensitively berates him for failing to video-record her appearance, an outburst that ruins the evening and embarrasses everyone present. That night as Peter questions her about her job, he seems nervous about what her answers might reveal, both curious and fearful of this insight into her work, and into Tennison herself.

51

The fate of their doomed relationship is sealed when Tennison fails to return home on time to cook dinner for Peter's business clients after lingering on the case in Oldham. Rather than catching an earlier train back to London she instead invites the prostitutes she is interviewing to come for a drink. Peter tells her angrily, 'Just once I wanted you to do something for me … . It's always you isn't it Jane? … . You don't care about anything else. No I'm wrong … . You care about your lads, you care about your rapists and your tarts'. The next day when she returns from work the flat is dark, still, and his things are gone. In stark contrast to this, the solitary life that she has embarked on, her answer-machine then plays back a message from her mum announcing that her sister has had a baby girl. From herein a pattern commences which has long been the fate of the workaholic cop and which will be followed throughout the series, in which Tennison is allowed short-term relationships and lovers, but never the prospect of a lasting, supportive relationship.

The closest she comes to such a partnership is with Dr Patrick Schofield (Stuart Wilson), the psychiatrist she meets in *Prime Suspect 4: The Lost Child* while investigating a paedophile suspect. By *Prime Suspect 4: The Scent of Darkness* the two are in a fully fledged relationship. Lying in bed contentedly with him one morning, she exclaims 'Let's not go in today … let's go for a walk on Parliament Hill … I mean it'. But this romantic scenario is an impossible one for Tennison. When Patrick agrees she capitulates, unable to let her private life take precedence over work commitments, exclaiming 'Oh God, you know I can't'. In a vulnerable moment she admits, 'This is the first time in my life I've had the feeling that I don't want to get up and go to work … . I don't want to screw up another relationship … . Tell me it's not going to happen'. But when we cut from their bedroom to a scene of the police turning up on the doorstep of a missing schoolgirl, the implication is that another '[screwed]-up relationship' is exactly what will follow. Tennison starts to believe that she is just an intriguing case study for Schofield and that he is collaborating with an investigative journalist to write a destructive exposé of her. Her suspicions are quickly

'I don't want to screw up another relationship': but things soon go wrong with Patrick Schofield

proved unfounded but the damage to their relationship is done. During a furious argument Schofield tells her what she surely already knows but cannot change, '[You] are never going to sort out any of your relationships until you find some way of separating your private life from your work'.

By *Prime Suspect 5: Errors of Judgement* her relationship with Schofield is over. Tennison has moved to a new job in Manchester following a climactic showdown with Thorndike in front of his Masonic friends at the end of *The Scent of Darkness*, in which she tells him she won't be driven out of her job and throws a glass of wine over him. The new series nevertheless begins with a promising sense of optimism. As it opens, Tennison wakes in her new home, walks out onto her rooftop terrace and surveys the horizon of her new city with apparent satisfaction. But she soon experiences friction with some of her new team and embarks on another ill-judged affair with a colleague, this time sleeping with her married boss, DCS Ballinger (John McArdle), shortly after starting her job. The credibility of their relationship is once more hindered by a weak script, with exchanges between the lovers that seem lifted from a Jackie Collins novel ('Jane, all I wanted to say was last night for me, it was electrifying! … Jesus Jane, I want you now!' he tells a somewhat bemused Tennison the morning after the night before).

In the course of her first case Tennison exposes Ballinger as having collaborated with a local gangster, 'The Street' (Steven Mackintosh), swapping police tip-offs for information in order to 'contain' crime and improve the district's crime statistics. Realising that he has betrayed her and all the principles she holds dear, the final scene finishes on a freeze-frame of Tennison's face as The Street lies dead, shot by armed-response officers, and Ballinger blithely admits his culpability before driving away with impunity. 'You bastard!' she rails at Ballinger. 'You compromise, and you deal and you bargain, until there's no law,

Tennison confronts her boss and lover DCS Ballinger, the corrupt cop in *Errors of Judgement*

there's no order, there's no justice. There's just some kind of messed-up secret society that you think you can control!' Tennison is left by the end seeming more alone than ever. Not only has she been deceived by Ballinger, she has misjudged her team, wrongly suspecting Devanney of being the 'leak'. It seems the 'Errors of Judgement' alluded to in the title are hers as much as Ballinger's.

While the romantic ineptitude of the lone detective may be a familiar scenario from Sam Spade to Inspector Morse, its implications shift when the cop in question is female, since it means that her very being and legitimacy as a woman becomes the subject of enquiry. The male officers surrounding Tennison continually comment on her relative attractiveness and speculate about her sexuality. 'I couldn't do it, couldn't, could you? A woman like Tennison', DC Growse (Anthony Audenshaw) ponders in *Prime Suspect 5*. 'As fast as you could throw her under me' his colleague replies. Even Devanney joins in this laddish objectification of Tennison, making the others laugh with her impersonation of Tennison in the pub, where she mimics her saying 'I screwed my way to the top!' No such scrutiny is exacted on the desirability and masculinity of the male cop who remains single and without a family of his own. Interestingly, in contrast to Tennison a number of her male colleagues are shown to be married or to have children; DCI Shefford sings 'Happy Birthday' to his son down the phone at the morgue; DI Burkin (who is later reprimanded for 'fraternising' with prostitutes) mutters in the office one evening that he can't stay late because, 'The wife's mother is staying with us'; Haskons (Richard Hawley) can't join Tennison for a drink after work as he's got to get home to his young twins. These moments both emphasise Tennison's comparative lack again and underline that whatever progress Equal Opportunities legislation may have brought, the choice between a policing career *or* a family life apparently remains an overwhelmingly female dilemma.

In the same vein, when Jonesy picks up Tennison in the early morning the day after their extended trip to Oldham and her failure to cook for Peter's colleagues, he complains that his wife '[gave him] an

earful' for coming home late to a congealed dinner. Tennison is not
sympathetic, responding brusquely that at least he has a wife to cook for
him, whereas she has to look after herself. Supper for Tennison seems
typically to consist of a glass or two of wine and a microwave meal.
In *Prime Suspect 2* it is up to Bob Oswalde to make her a proper meal at
home after he comes round to find she's planning to have 'one of those
frozen chilli-con-carne things' for the second night running. A bare
fridge twinned with a compensatory bottle of booze constitutes another
well-established trope of the single cop's empty home life, reiterating the
sacrifices he's made for the job while also alluding to his dependency on
alcohol. Hints that Tennison may have a drink problem build steadily as
the series progresses, from her playful behest to Oswalde in *Prime
Suspect 2* that they should 'drink everything in the mini-bar' of their
hotel room to the grim contents of her shopping basket in *Inner Circles*
– a bundle of ready meals and two bottles of whisky. Her reliance on the
comfort of alcohol advances more or less in tandem with her career,
until by *The Final Act* she is compelled to join Alcoholics Anonymous.
But here again, Tennison's penchant for booze and her ineptitude in the
kitchen signal something more than tropes of the classic maverick cop.
Her inability to cook adequately points again to her deficiencies in the
domestic arena and underlines her failure as a 'proper' woman, the
flipside of her success as a woman cop.

Conspirators and Victims: Crime Drama's 'Other Women'

While women police officers had been largely absent in TV crime drama
prior to the 1980s they had fulfilled other roles as criminal conspirators
and victims, and continued to do so after the growth of television's
women cops. Provocatively, in the first *Prime Suspect* there is a
discomforting narrative thread which suggests *female* complicity in
Marlow's crimes. This is a motif that has again informed the
dissemination of many real-life crimes where women have featured

either as a suspected accomplice or gullible 'stooge' to a prolific male serial killer. In the UK, such cases have included the Fred and Rose West case, where in 1994 the husband and wife serial killers were found responsible between them for the murder of at least twelve women. In the Yorkshire Ripper case, Peter Sutcliffe's wife Sonia became the subject of intense media scrutiny following his arrest in 1981, as disbelief met her claim that she'd never suspected him of involvement in the murders of thirteen women. Alternatively, domineering mothers are often depicted as the root cause of the male psychopath, a scenario of female accountability which neatly describes the psychology attributed to George Marlow. His apparently unhealthy attachment to his crudely over-made-up mother and the uncomfortably flirtatious relationship they appear to enjoy when he visits her at her residential home, suggest she is in some way complicit in his horribly warped perception of women. Interestingly, the most flamboyant shot of the first series is given over to capturing the special relationship between them, as they sing together on the pier and the camera swoops away high above them into an aerial shot until they are two tiny figures alone together in the landscape.

These nagging doubts about Marlow's mother are confirmed in *Prime Suspect 4: The Scent of Darkness* when Tennison is forced to review the Marlow case after new victims evidencing his *modus operandi* begin to appear and the soundness of his conviction comes under question. Once again fighting to save her career and integrity under the gaze of Thorndike and others who would relish seeing her reputation destroyed, Tennison is eventually vindicated when it transpires that one of Marlow's prison guards is copycatting his crimes. But her new investigation also uncovers the details of Marlow's darkly Oedipal past. When Tennison quizzes Marlow's mother she learns that as a young lad he'd witnessed her adultery during a secret tryst on the beach. In ghoulish devotion Marlow later sprayed his mother's perfume, a gift from her lover, on his victims.

Meanwhile, the representation of Marlow's girlfriend Moyra as a harping 'hard-nosed bitch', a wilful if ultimately repentant and

57

As Marlow serenades his mother, the two are dramatically captured together
in an elaborate aerial shot

misguided accessory who gives Marlow a false alibi, means that she is
also made to share a measure of blame for the murders. Moyra's silence,
her suppression of the fact that he had at one time enacted sexual
aggression on her, 'enables' Marlow to kill again. The relationship
between her and Tennison is fraught from the outset when on meeting
Tennison, she shows an acerbic grasp of the popular role of women cops
by asking her caustically 'What have they sent you for? The female
touch is it? Soften me up?' In many ways the most disturbing scene in
Prime Suspect comes close to the end when Tennison is interviewing
Moyra, who at this point has still refused to break her alibi for Marlow.
Tennison demands that Moyra admit she had known the victims, Karen
Howard and Della Mornay, pulling out Della's police mug-shot. Moyra
refuses to look. Tennison pulls out a close-up of Della's corpse, her
decomposing face, then another of Karen tied up and bloodied on the
floor. In the harsh, unforgiving light of the interview room, though, we

linger not on these pictures but on Moyra's face refusing to look. Tennison grows frustrated and she demands angrily, 'Look. Look! Hands tied behind her back. Look at the marks on her body. Look at her, Moyra!' As Tennison and Moyra's lawyer begin to bicker among themselves, Moyra finally looks.

We cut to the photos of the corpses laid out on the desk as Moyra's manicured and bejewelled hand reaches out to touch Della's face and rests on it. The image is a disconcerting one, the juxtaposition of living flesh against the dead and decaying, the carefully groomed against the hideously defiled, an intimate gesture against brutal violence. Moyra speaks at last: 'Get them to leave' she says of the men. There is an odd appeal made in this moment to a kind of female solidarity, despite the gulf that exists between Moyra and the police. In wanting to exclude the men from the room Moyra reverses the exclusion Tennison has suffered so many times with her male colleagues. With just Tennison and Havers present, Moyra finally opens up.

'Look at her!': Moyra touches the photos of Marlow's victims

Victim or accessory to murder?: Moyra breaks down during questioning

'He did it to me once. But I ... I didn't like it. Tied my hands ... leather straps'. She breaks off and starts to gag and choke. Yet Tennison watches her without flinching; there is a virtually imperceptible flicker across her face that just might suggest exasperation. She then turns to Maureen and looks at her as if to say, 'This is it!' Maureen too is silent, but an instinctual exchange between them is apparent as she gives the faintest of nods and smiles. There is female camaraderie at last in this room, the understanding that Moyra had apparently appealed to. But it is a bond that Moyra is very much excluded from. As Tennison and Maureen leave Moyra retching without comment to share a moment of silent vindication, their exchange of looks suggests a victory of sorts, but one rendered hollow by the manner in which it was won.

This is at once a brilliant and deeply disturbing scene for the ambivalent position it takes on all the women present. Should we feel contempt or understanding for Tennison and Havers's response? Have the police turned these women into something so horribly unfeeling, so driven only by 'masculine' vindication that they can revel in their own victory in the face of human collapse? Are they police officers first and women second? Is that the way it should be? And finally, should we loathe or pity Moyra – for isn't she a victim in all this too? In Oldham, the prostitutes told Tennison that Jeannie, the first young prostitute Marlow murdered, 'Never stood a chance. Her foster dad was screwing her at seven. She was out on the streets at fourteen'. In this interview we learn that Moyra was also on the streets as a young woman, appearing on charges of soliciting with Della in Manchester Juvenile Court in 1976. This history situates Moyra as sharing an affinity with the dead prostitutes, though it is not suggested visually as with Tennison, who is recurrently framed against pictures of the victims' corpses in the incident room. Rather their affinity lies in their shared social position, their stories of male aggression, sex, class and powerlessness, which blur the lines of Moyra's culpability for Marlow's crimes.

Don't Look Now

An insistence on looking, or a refusal to look, at women – more specifically at Tennison and the spectacle proffered by the female corpses – is marked as a central motif in the original *Prime Suspect*'s gendered aesthetics and its investigation of male power. The series foregrounded the act of looking as one that holds peculiarly potent significance in terms of *recognising* women, in both senses of the word – that is, in naming and identifying women *and* in acknowledging their position and accomplishments. The disastrous start to the first investigation is caused by Shefford's refusal or inability to look at the corpse, leading to the misidentification of Karen's body as Della's. At the murder scene, as the pathologist Felix (Bryan Pringle) examines the body, he asks, 'John, do you want a look?', but Shefford shakes his head and lingers by the doorway. Later, as Felix performs the post-mortem, he comments 'Her whole body's badly bruised with extensive bruising to

the vagina – want to see?', and again Shefford shakes his head and
moves away. It later becomes clear that his reluctance to look at her
springs partly from his having been sexually involved with Della, and
that he and other officers have enjoyed liaisons with prostitutes as a
perk of the job. But more broadly this refusal to 'see' Karen is part of a
larger narrative motif running throughout the programme. It is only
when Tennison takes over the case that anyone 'sees' the victim for the
first time, not as a collection of injuries and evidence, not as an
opportunity to break Paxman's record for the fastest arrest on a murder
inquiry, but as a woman whom the others have failed to recognise. Later,
when Della's body is found dumped on Sunningdale golf course, in the
hellish thick of the mud, darkness and rain, Tennison goes to the officer
at the scene and says 'I'd like to have a look please'. He is reticent and
patronising – 'Are you sure? It's not a pretty sight'. Tennison is
forthright – 'I want to see her face'. In a shocking, rotten, terrible image,
the earth is rubbed away from the corpse's nose and eye sockets to reveal

While the men are frequently shot together as an imposing group, Tennison 63
is framed alone in front of the victims' pictures

her face. Tennison recognises her instantly, nods and stands; 'That's
Della Mornay'.

There is a gendered matrix of looking and seeing at work in
this, first, pivoting around who can and can't 'see' both the victims and
Tennison and, second, regarding who will meet Tennison's gaze.
Looking is inscribed as an empowering act for men who can withhold or
grant the gaze, and the recognition it carries, on women. This is a
process that does not operate in quite the same way as the objectifying
male gaze at the heart of classical Hollywood cinema, since it is not
always constructed as pivoting on sexually motivated voyeurism. But it
is nevertheless a system of looks that is equally embedded in gender and
power. Like the victims, Tennison endures a series of encounters where
men refuse to look at her, undermining her presence and position as a
means of disempowering her. Karen's father Major Howard and her

boyfriend Michael (Ralph Fiennes); DS Eastel (Dave Bond) at the Sunningdale crime scene; the policeman in Manchester – all choose in some way not to look at Tennison, typically 'recognising', gravitating to or addressing the other, less senior, but crucially *male* officer with her.

A similar gendered dichotomy is to be found in the recurrent ways in which the male officers and Tennison are oppositionally framed and shot. The men's solidarity is underlined by the manner in which they are repeatedly grouped together in the canteen and incident room by an expansive, circular, panning or tracking camera movement, technically difficult scenes which required a good deal of preparatory setting-up time. In contrast we frequently see Tennison isolated and/or on one side of the incident room framed against the photos of the victims in still, medium close-up, so she is symbolically aligned with these dead women rather than with her male colleagues. While later series would not pursue this distinctive tracking camera movement in this manner, the use of the still close-up on Tennison would remain a hallmark of the series' sombre and reflective tone. Later, in the opening scenes of *Prime Suspect 6: The Last Witness*, the visual parallel between Tennison and her woman victims is returned to and made even more explicit. Following the discovery of another dead and tortured female corpse, this time dumped on a building site, we cut to a series of close-ups of a woman's body being inspected on a white sheet. Our presumption that we have cut to the morgue is proved wrong when it gradually becomes clear that this body is alive and we are actually watching Tennison's latest health exam. In a series of dislocated close-ups of her hands, torso and feet, which foreshadow the post-mortem that awaits the victim's body, she too is subjected to the processes of medicalised annotation and scrutiny. The scene acts as a reminder of her own vulnerable (and ageing) female body, not least because the results of the exam may be used to push her into retirement.

The continued use of the still camera on a solitary Tennison throughout the first *Prime Suspect* underlines her difference, contrasting with the recurrent bravura camera movement across a brooding sea of men. But intriguingly, Tennison is ultimately

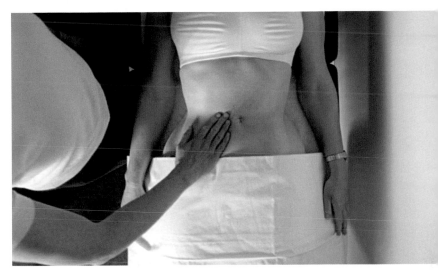

Under scrutiny: Tennison's health exam at the start of *The Last Witness* foreshadows the autopsy of the victim

incorporated into the expansive, 'masculine', panning camera at the end, when the men surround her with flowers, champagne and singing in the incident room following Marlow's confession. The camera surveys them in a circular movement as they toast her jubilantly at their centre in a particularly elaborate and challenging Steadicam shot which necessitated a long day's shoot.[39] At one level, Tennison's response – 'You bastards. I thought you'd all pissed off home' – appears to suggest that she has finally become one of the lads, adopting their language and winning acceptance from them as they laugh and cheer alongside her. Alternatively, Glen Creeber sees the scene as one which suggests not the incorporation of Tennison into 'masculine' behavioural traits but the men's recognition, finally, of her femininity; 'The fizzy champagne covers her and all the male officers with white froth and light, the flowers she is given a symbolic triumph of the "natural" and the "feminine" over the "urban", "masculine" and neo-noir world'.[40]

A celebration or reminder of male dominance? – Tennison is sprayed with champagne by the team after Marlow confesses

But one might also read a hint of menace into these images. Tennison seems almost engulfed by the men when the camera circles around them dizzily, as if trapped in an eerie, overwhelming merry-go-ground. A psychoanalytic reading of the men could make much of their spraying her with popping champagne bottles as a symbolically aggressive act which connotes sexual dominance over her. This is a victorious moment but, as the series would go on to show again, Tennison is still far from comfortably affiliated into this world. Admittedly she will win some allies over time, with Haskons and 'Taff' DS Simms (Robert Pugh) proving particularly loyal to her. But even while she solves the case here and throughout later series, there is often an accompanying sense of open-endedness to the narratives of *Prime Suspect*. The final scenes recurrently seem to undermine Tennison's achievements and render the endings comparatively dark. After all her labour to secure his confession, George Marlow changes his plea to 'Not guilty' at the end of the first series; in the final scene of *Inner Circles* her resolve to quit smoking weakens and she cadges a cigarette from Chris; at the end of *Prime Suspect 5* DCS Ballinger walks away scot-free despite her having exposed his alliance with a psychopathic gangster. All this serves to reinforce the programme's sombre tone since it suggests both that the work of the detective is never (and can never) be complete, just as Tennison's place in the masculine order of the police will never finally be won.

While the complex characterisation of its woman protagonist and the programme's scrutiny of gender in crime drama ensured its place in television history, these were not the only facets of *Prime Suspect* which broke new ground or courted controversy. So too did its graphic representation of the corpse and its co-opting of the growth of forensic science constitute innovative material that would go on to become standard features of TV crime fiction as it progressed into the 1990s. With this in mind, in the next chapter, I look further at where *Prime Suspect*'s reputation for 'gritty realism' sprang from and trace how it took crime drama into the autopsy rooms and science labs in new and compelling ways.

67

3 Reimagining Realism: Murder, Forensics and the Body in *Prime Suspect*

TV crime series have long claimed a rather privileged relationship with 'the real' and in this regard *Prime Suspect* was like many of its predecessors, heralded in their time for having captured an authentic vision of police work. But the parameters of how realism is signalled are not fixed. Instead audiences and the media are constantly renegotiating expectations and signifiers of what constitutes 'the real' and in this respect *Prime Suspect* was at the vanguard of a period of reinvention for crime-drama realism in the 1990s.

One of the ways in which *Prime Suspect* underscored its critical awareness of the entangled relationship between realism/the media/crime fiction was through representing the media *within* its own narratives. By embedding the role of the media within a number of storylines, its portrayals of television and the press became one of the markers of its realism. In the first *Prime Suspect*, for example, we see Tennison made the subject of a Sunday tabloid spread after George Marlow appears to have sold his story to the papers, claiming 'he is being hounded by an obsessive woman'. Later, in *Prime Suspect 2*, she becomes the focus of a tabloid 'exposé' again when she is secretly photographed outside her home embracing Bob Oswalde. Examining the reciprocal relationship between police and media, *Prime Suspect* explores both how the media report crime sensationally and how the police use the media for their own ends through press conferences and appeals, with DCS Ballinger particularly fancying himself as media-savvy. Both the first series and *Prime Suspect 5*, for example, feature Tennison excitedly appearing on live television to appeal for public help on *Crime Night*. In a thinly veiled pastiche of the British crime reconstruction programme, *Crimewatch*, the series highlights the formulaic manner in which such popular appeal programmes operate. Furthermore, when the Marlow case is picked up by *Crime Night* Tennison is visibly thrilled, not just by the opportunity to utilise the reach of television to publicise the case, but by the validation it brings to her personally; 'I'm going to be the first woman DCI ever on *Crime Night*!', she announces proudly, welcoming the momentary celebrity this will bring. These various reflexive and intertextual exchanges

Tennison makes her second appearance on *Crime Night* in *Errors of Judgement*

underline *Prime Suspect*'s awareness of the interdependent but often fraught relationship between the police and media, at the same time amplifying the series' own participation in this relationship.

    Prime Suspect's drive to reimagine cop-show realism was made instantly apparent from the opening credits which marked the series' stark, sombre style by silently announcing Helen Mirren's name and the series title in simple white-on-black titles.[41] In the next shot the audience is delivered straight into the drama with a high-angled view of a rainy night-time street outside the first crime scene. The credits' simple monochrome design, and the speed with which we cut from these fleeting titles into the unfolding action, would become a hallmark of later series, signalling immediately that *Prime Suspect* would be a dark, hard-hitting crime drama. Press coverage quickly situated the series as having shaken up the tired generic formulae of the cop series. The *Sunday Times*, for example, called it 'one of the grittiest and most gripping dramas of recent memory' and noted that 'what separated *Prime Suspect* from a thousand US cop shows [was] its realism. The unearthed bodies looked all too much like unearthed bodies ... the police procedure had almost documentary conviction'.[42] More than any other term, the word 'gritty' has become a byword among television commentators for tough, challenging drama and it was used with conspicuous frequency across the reception of *Prime Suspect*. Interestingly, the *Sunday Times* reviewer also drew on the gravitas of documentary to describe the series, bestowing the 'truth claims' and (high-culture) critical esteem enjoyed by the documentary genre onto a (low-culture) fictional police procedural. Writing in the *Daily Mail*, Peter Paterson observed in the same vein that Tennison was 'certainly more believable, somehow, than the stereotypes one recalls from *The Gentle Touch* and *Juliet Bravo* ... this was a hard, gritty, realistic murder story which was sometimes over-zealous in showing us the grisly evidence'.[43] Comparing it to other contemporaneous series, director Christopher Menaul emphasised *Prime Suspect*'s sombre realism by situating it as a 'perfect antidote' to the 'glossy' TV 'tecs of the moment, Morse, Poirot and Sherlock Holmes'.[44] Such descriptions signal again how realism is often negotiated more in relation to other programmes than to the 'real world' itself.

Significantly, both the *Sunday Times* and *Daily Mail* reviews also point to *Prime Suspect*'s push to 'show us' or make visible what had typically been kept out of sight in crime fiction, as the camera lingered on the scene-of-crime photos and mortuary slabs that were once kept peripheral. In this respect it was no surprise that *Prime Suspect*'s 'unnecessarily explicit visual details of a dead body' along with its 'strong language' prompted ten complaints to the then-Broadcasting Standards Council (BSC). Defending itself in a statement issued in response to the complaints, Granada Television observed

> it was the company's intention to be as *honest and authentic* about the professional and public impact of a case which was distressing and disturbing ... the production team attempted to make a compromise between the *extreme realism of a similar situation in real-life* and undue sanitisation (emphasis added).[45]

Neither complaint, of undue visual or verbal explicitness, was upheld. The BSC Complaints Committee found that the strong language was not inappropriate 'in the context of a play giving a realistic account of police investigations' and, although it recognised 'the grimness of the spectacle of the bodies displayed', it found the images 'did not exceed limits reasonable in a drama of this sort'.

Interesting details emerge from the BSC report. Granada Television defends itself against charges of 'unnecessary explicit[ness]' by claiming the series was prompted by a serious, conscientious desire for 'honesty' and 'authenticity' and to do justice to 'real life'. The BSC's findings are also revealing, indicating the fraught ground crime drama often treads between 'fiction' and 'realism' by referring to the series as delivering 'a realistic account', but also being variously a 'drama' and 'play'. This last description, situating the miniseries as 'a play', is particularly telling. Production of the single television play has declined greatly over the past three decades but it had traditionally been seen as

71

the zenith of intelligent, accomplished programming, conferring a certain cultural prestige on television as a whole. Like those reviews that described the programme as 'documentary-like', the description of *Prime Suspect* as a 'play' in formal terms is a revealing choice of words; it adds dramatic weight and loftiness to the programme's profile and points to the earnestness with which *Prime Suspect* was received.

In what follows I examine in more detail the claims that *Prime Suspect* crafted new modes of realism in crime drama, looking particularly at the original series which I argue set a benchmark for the genre thereafter. At one level, it played with familiar territory by drawing on some of the established crime-drama conventions of film noir. For example, swathed in a ritzy fur coat and heavy make-up while brandishing a cigarette, Moyra carries clear visual associations of the genre's deadly femme fatale or 'spider woman'. Elsewhere, Glen Creeber has suggested that even the name 'Marlow' signals the series'

Cigarettes and shadows: the series' visual echoes of film noir are clear as Tennison anxiously watches Marlow's identity parade

indebtedness to classical noir since it is 'unmistakably reminiscent of Raymond Chandler's fictional hero Philip Marlowe'.[46]

But equally the series' reception as a 'hard, gritty, realistic' drama was achieved in part by other distinctive and edgy stylistic motifs, such as the shaky camera in the early scene-of-crime sequences; the harsh, fluorescent lighting of the station's interior scenes and the recurrent use of muffled, overlapping sound. Throughout *Prime Suspect* the audience must frequently strain to hear dialogue over the background noise of the busy open-plan office, an effective technique in demanding viewers' complete concentration. When Havers first voices her suspicions about Moyra's work as a beautician, for example, not even Tennison can hear her above the office chatter and she must call for quiet as the surrounding noise tapers off and gradually, she, we and the rest of the team hear what Havers has to say. The cast have described how director Menaul drew on theatrical techniques to achieve the frenetic atmosphere of the incident room, encouraging the actors to improvise the interludes framing the script. His approach accounts for those recurrent instances where the actors walk and stand in front of each other in the office, and the sense of a constant, ad-libbed background murmur that accompanies these scenes.[47] Though it was not adopted in later episodes, this 'authentic' layering of sound still stands up as one of the most accomplished and distinctive aspects of the original series.

However, in order to examine *Prime Suspect*'s realism I do not wish to focus only on its aesthetic innovations. Rather, I wish to argue also that part of the reason the first *Prime Suspect* struck such a cultural chord, in Britain particularly, was its evocation of high-profile news stories and real-life cases resonant in the public imagination. These included not only Alison Halford's sexual discrimination case against the Merseyside Police, but also the infamous 'Yorkshire Ripper' serial murders of the 1970s and 80s. In its portrayal of Marlow as an 'ordinary' likeable man just like the 'Ripper' Peter Sutcliffe, and its depiction of police bungling and contempt for prostitutes, the programme seemed to mirror deeply disconcerting but well-documented aspects of what was at the time the biggest manhunt ever undertaken by British police. This willingness to engage with, and even pre-empt, controversial and discomforting aspects of contemporary British policing and culture was also true of later instalments. As Julia Hallam points out, *Prime Suspect 2*'s exploration of police racism and scenes of a young black man found dead in his cell predated Sir William Macpherson's 1999 report on the Stephen Lawrence Inquiry which found the Metropolitan Police guilty of 'institutional racism',[48] 'but not the growing swell of disquiet in the media concerning the numbers of young black men dying in police custody'.[49] *Prime Suspect 3* focused on the underground lives and abuse endured by London's rent boys, both on the streets and as children in care. In this plot, Hallam argues, 'the contemporary dimensions of [the] story are drawn from accounts of male rape in local authority children's homes that led to the eventual closure of numerous institutions in England and Wales', following investigations such as Operation Care in Merseyside in 1997.[50] Later still, *Prime Suspect 6: The Last Witness* tapped into the moral panic over immigration, in particular fears of Eastern Europeans alleged to be members of a 'Balkan mafia'. When Tennison takes over the investigation into the torture and murder of Samira Blekic, a young Bosnian Muslim woman, the case leads her into an underworld of exploited immigrant labour and exposes the cover-up of a wartime massacre in Bosnia. In her quest for justice it is not merely clandestine deal-making at New Scotland Yard and 'media hysteria', as she puts it, that she must confront, but the prejudice of her own officers ('Country's sinking under the weight of them' mutters Taff stonily on seeing a crowd of immigrant men jostling for work as casual labour).

Quite beyond its particular appeal to UK audiences, however, the original *Prime Suspect* also spoke to international audiences through its innovative engagement with the development of forensic techniques in criminal investigations. Coming just a few years after the first breakthroughs in DNA fingerprinting, the programme broke new ground in its use of modern forensic terminology, opening up the spaces of the autopsy room and the forensic labs in novel ways that now form the cornerstone of much contemporary crime drama. This shift has not been unproblematic; just as *Prime Suspect* prompted complaints to the BSC, commentators have observed since then that the use of ever-more explicit images of victims has become a perturbing motif played for cheap shock value, and to capitalise on the possibilities afforded by CGI, rather than a marker of the genre's maturity (with *CSI* being a notable case in point). How did *Prime Suspect* put these changes in the substance of crime drama in motion and where did its claims to be 'honest' and 'authentic' lie?

'He's a Really Friendly Bloke': Murder and the 'Everyman'

One of the most intriguing 'realist' aspects of the original *Prime Suspect* lay instantly in the characterisation of its killer as an amiable, attractive, regular man on the street, in contrast to more sensationalist representations of this figure. Marlow is arguably most interesting, paradoxical though it may seem, for being so undistinguished, since it is precisely his seeming banality that makes him such a thought-provoking, unsettling and 'truthful' villain. Marlow's status as 'Everyman' rather than a patently deviant or marginalised figure was crucial to the series' impact and reception. Once again, La Plante reimagined the template of much crime fiction, constructing a serial killer who isn't transparently odd or a loner, but rather who is in a long-term relationship, has a steady job where he is well liked and a mother who, however eccentric she may be, has evidently been a loving parent. Marlow's boss at the paint factory where he works as a salesman explains he stood by him on a previous rape charge as he couldn't quite believe he'd done it; how could a 'good-looking bloke' like George who 'always had girls coming on to him' be a rapist? Marlow is popular, charming, unassuming and gregarious, a 'normal' man in every aspect of his outward appearance, to the extent that even the undercover police watching his house can't help but warm to him. 'He's a really friendly

The serial killer as Everyman: Marlow chats with the undercover detectives outside his home

bloke, chats to us every day', remarks a perplexed DC Rosper (Andrew Tiernan), struggling to reconcile the casual bonhomie he shares with George with his expectations of what a serial killer should be like. And although Marlow admits to paying for sex, in the homosocial world of *Prime Suspect* this isn't particularly unusual or transgressive, since it emerges that numerous police officers including Shefford enjoy 'off-duty leg-overs' with prostitutes. Marlow himself seems to presume this is a pastime they share when he describes to Shefford how he picked up a prostitute and notes in a confidential fashion, 'Well, you know they like to hustle as much out of you as they can'.

Significantly also, *Prime Suspect*'s slow-paced digressions away from the spaces of the murder inquiry itself into the private sphere of the home extend not just to Tennison's domestic life but – more radically – to Marlow's too. He is seen more than once in his comfortable home with his common-law wife Moyra, who is clearly a devoted homemaker. These domestic exchanges work to humanise Marlow further and integrate him into the fabric of a common social world. The scene in which he proposes to Moyra quietly conveys the real warmth and companionship of their relationship. As she drinks the tea he's just brought her, he goes down on one knee before her to tell her he loves her and they kiss with genuine affection. Even the cosy colour palette of the scene underlines its sense of intimacy; coded together in creams and blues, the couple complement the comfortable interiors of their living room in an image of homely contentedness. Moyra's affection for Marlow, and his desirability, is evident not only in her loyalty to him but in the quietly observed scene in which she stands by the window in the dark smoking and looking at him in bed, before climbing in beside him and tenderly caressing his back, initiating their lovemaking. Such a killer is far more 'dangerous' than the more familiar serial murderers of popular cinema, outsiders who are marked by palpable social or physical inadequacy. Instead, in *Prime Suspect* there is

Home comforts: Marlow and Moyra relax together in their cosy lounge

an implicit suggestion that, like an unmarked police car, men resembling George could be anywhere, moving unseen among us. Misogyny lies in the mundane, the programme suggests, the easy dismissal of women as 'tarts' and 'slags' that we witness from the male police officers, as much as in the spectacular excess of George's crimes. The difference is one of degree rather than nature.

Dissecting the Ripper Myth

In many of these details, the representation of Marlow and the events of the murder inquiry in *Prime Suspect* seemed to mirror aspects of the UK's notorious Yorkshire Ripper case. La Plante has made the link explicit in interview, remarking of Marlow that, 'Because he was a plausible liar, everyone wanted to believe him. Well, the Yorkshire Ripper was a plausible liar; they had him in five times and let him go'.[51] In fact, Peter Sutcliffe was interviewed and released on nine occasions, walking away each time in a series of blunders that subsequently led to condemnation of the chronic mismanagement of the case. Sutcliffe first committed murder in October 1975, striking again three months later in January 1976. Since both victims had worked as prostitutes, the West Yorkshire police quickly and mistakenly presumed that they had a 'prostitute killer' on their hands. The press then promptly announced that 'a "Jack the Ripper Killer" was on the loose',[52] invoking one of the most notorious (and still unsolved) murder cases in British history.

Sutcliffe was finally arrested in January 1981 after a random police check revealed false number plates on his car (while in a further parallel Marlow's car also proves to be his downfall). By this time he had murdered thirteen women across the towns and cities of northern England. That he was able to do so can be at least partly accounted for by the ineptitude and misogyny of many of those involved in the investigation and by the wholly unanticipated *ordinariness* of 'The Ripper'. Sutcliffe was an unassuming married man living in a semi-detached house in a respectable Yorkshire suburb and hence simply not what anyone had imagined or looked for. Much like the affable, similarly settled George Marlow, one of the most perturbing features of the Sutcliffe case was precisely the 'revelation' that far from announcing himself through his sheer peculiarity, the serial killer could be the guy next door, your work colleague, the man sitting next to you on the bus – an ordinary man.[53]

The similarity Sutcliffe (like Marlow) bore to other 'ordinary men' was underlined by the manner in which some police on the inquiry (again, like those investigating Marlow) expressed similarly misogynistic 'common-sense' views about women and prostitutes. In both the real-life case and TV fiction, women were categorised differently by the police officers working the investigation according to whether they were 'innocent victims' or prostitutes. The same prejudices are still at work in *Prime Suspect 2* after Joanne Fagunwa's unidentified remains are found and Muddyman tells Tennison, 'I don't know what you're so bothered about, it's just another runaway, another dead prostitute'. For at least some of the Yorkshire Ripper team, the murder of 'ordinary' women had moved the case into a whole new league, transforming it into a much more serious matter, for wasn't it understandable, normal even, to despise prostitutes? As one senior detective put it in a 1979 press conference: 'He has made it clear he hates prostitutes. Many people do. We, as a police force will continue to arrest prostitutes. But the Ripper is now killing *innocent girls* (emphasis added).[54] It is difficult not to see echoes here of the prostitutes in Oldham who tell Tennison how arbitrarily the male officers investigated the murder of their friend Jeannie: 'They never gave a shit about Jeannie. We're rubbish. Until they want a jerk-off'. The local police sergeant bears this out; 'Slags isn't the word for them' he tells Tennison contemptuously at the abandoned factory where Jeannie was brutally murdered. It seems telling also that Tennison's investigation into Marlow's early attacks takes her to the north of England, to Oldham, as if symbolically into the territory that the Yorkshire Ripper had also roamed. The men are two of a kind, sharing a deadly disdain for women which is revealed to be all too close to the scornful attitudes of the very men investigating them.

79

From Deduction to DNA: Science and the New Tools of Crime Drama

If the Marlow case seemed to draw on recent crime history, the series' evocation of scientific breakthroughs in criminal investigation looked very much to the present and future. The years immediately prior to *Prime Suspect* had seen dramatic discoveries in genetic research that would forever change the uses of forensic evidence within criminal justice and which, therefore, would also inevitably come to alter the landscape of TV crime drama. In September 1984, researcher Alec Jeffreys at the University of Leicester discovered the existence of DNA 'fingerprints' which could reveal the genetic code unique to every individual. The potential uses for this science were soon apparent: paternity testing; immigration disputes; species conservation and classification; and, of course, crime. DNA fingerprinting opened up the possibility that trace evidence such as semen or hair left by the perpetrator at a crime scene could be used for identification (or elimination) with a degree of certainty hitherto unimagined. The speed and extent with which the technology would change the practice of criminal justice was not yet anticipated, but crime quickly became the arena in which advances in DNA research made the greatest impact. By 2005 Britain's National Criminal DNA Database contained some 3 million samples obtained from suspects and convicted criminals and 250,000 crime-scene samples.[55] DNA evidence is not infallible of course and has been associated with a number of miscarriages of justice, but public fascination with this new science was swift and has seemingly yet to abate. In a succession of new crime dramas from *Silent Witness* to *Waking the Dead* (BBC, 2000–) and *Dexter* (Showtime, 2006–), forensic science and scientists have taken centre-stage, often over and above the investigators to whom they were traditionally subordinate. This turn has been most spectacularly evident again in the huge success of the *CSI: Crime Scene Investigation* franchise since 2000. Indicating a move away from character-led drama, it has been said that *science* 'is the star of the show'. But this shift of focus in crime drama did not occur overnight and in this respect, *Prime Suspect* broke new ground. In fact, the series has even been credited with having featured 'the first time DNA had been mentioned on a TV show'.[56]

La Plante was one of the first crime dramatists to respond to the new prominence of forensic science in crime investigation and to tap into popular curiosity about it. In the first series she dared to counterbalance the tension and conflict of the incident and interview rooms with occasional, unexpected and quietly observed diversions into the police labs, or sequences of forensic teams collecting evidence. Enhancing the programme's 'quasi-documentary' sensibility,[57] the laboratory scenes had a kind of humdrum, fly-on-the-wall quality in which anonymous technicians were seen going about the unglamorous graft (in contrast to the gloss and suspense of *CSI*) of logging and examining evidence. These moments are devoid of 'drama' as such. They capture only perfunctory tasks and seemingly banal, brief exchanges of dialogue among peripheral characters, while other snatches of barely audible workplace discussion

81

The lab scenes gave a momentary glimpse into the labour behind forensics go on around them. Instead, these sequences give a 'behind-the-scenes' glimpse of the kind of methodical scientific work necessary to determine identification and secure convictions, labour which again had not typically been seen on screen.

The first of the lab sequences in *Prime Suspect* comes early in the drama, shortly after the discovery of Karen Howard's battered body. As the scene opens, a man in a white coat rips a page from a printer and strides over to a woman colleague announcing, 'Oh yes, this will narrow the field. Look what we've got here. Rare blood group, A/B secreter. That's 75 per cent of 3.2 per cent isn't it?' Together they work out some statistics using a calculator, and he concludes that the blood type could belong to one person in 2,500. The woman technician tells him 'We had some rare blood groups recorded when we started up the database. I'll have them check this one out', a reference to the recently established National DNA Database. Despite the hustle and bustle around the pair, which suggests just how industrious forensic labs are in supporting police work, it makes for a rather pedestrian scene, seemingly driven by a desire to impart some basic scientific information to the audience. It is oddly and rather disruptively situated, given that it comes so early in the episode and so close to the discovery of the body and all the pressing questions and suspicions this find brings. But these sequences of 'dead time', coming within a storyline and a genre typically driven by a sense of urgency, provide a new perspective on the processes of criminal investigation, one quite removed from the terrain of wailing sirens and screeching tyres. In including such labour in the storyline, these scenes bolstered *Prime Suspect*'s claims to have delivered a newly 'authentic' take on an established genre.

Bringing out the Dead: The Body in *Prime Suspect*

From the outset *Prime Suspect* was determined also to bring a greater degree of realism to its depiction of the corpse. As Shefford first enters the bedsit crime scene, the forensic pathologist, Felix, is already at work examining the victim's body. Her hands can be seen tied in plastic bags to preserve evidence that may be trapped under the nails, a small detail that constituted an attentive respect for crime-scene and forensic procedure. Felix speaks into a Dictaphone, narrating the body's injuries as he examines it. Drawing on a number of calculations, from the victim's rectal temperature and that of the room to the effect of the cold draught on the stairs, he is able to determine how long she has been lying dead there. As the corpse is turned over to transport it to the mortuary there is a close-up of the victim's horribly bloodied and bludgeoned face. Within moments of the series opening, then, the audience has already witnessed a startling degree of attention to forensic detail.

At the morgue shortly after, the victim's naked, mottled body is seen laid out on a gurney, surrounded by men dressed in scrubs, including Otley and Shefford, who nervously avoid looking down at her. As Felix lifts her hand to point to the 'nasty little nick' on her wrist, her mutilated right breast fills the frame behind. He systematically works his way through the injuries to the body while a series of close-ups capture his description. 'Clean entry wounds, some are up to six inches deep' he observes as we cut to the gashes to her torso. 'I reckon she's got semen in virtually every orifice' he concludes impassively. Clearly, this is not *Quincy, M.E.* and the body in *Prime Suspect* is treated throughout with similar frank visual and verbal explicitness. The corpse comes to act as a vivid signifier of the text's realism, but such images are inescapably contentious. While ostensibly claiming to be prompted by a desire for 'realism', they might also be accused of pandering to ghoulishness and of infusing the series with a deliberately provocative frisson of grisly voyeurism.

When Tennison, suspecting that Shefford has wrongly identified the body, first attends the morgue, her professionalism is marked by her willingness to examine the corpse thoroughly, something both Shefford and Jones fail to do. As Felix mentions the perforated eardrum caused 'by a blow to the side of the head here' she (and the camera) move in to look more closely. As she asks to see the cut to the

83

wrist and leans down to look, our impression is of someone working methodically through the evidence, seeking to understand the body before her rather than being repelled by it as Jonesy evidently is. When the real Della's body is found at the Sunningdale golf course, the officer on duty there is clearly surprised at Tennison's desire to inspect the filthy, decomposing body *in situ* and her confident identification of the victim. Without hesitation she bends down again to see the victim's face in close-up. As the dirt and mud are scraped from the face and the head is manoeuvred round for her (and thus the audience) to see in all its hideous detail, the body resembles something hardly human. But throughout the series, barring her evident discomfort at viewing the body of the murdered baby in *The Lost Child*, Tennison never exhibits revulsion or nervousness about the corpse.

In this respect, one of the most striking images Menaul constructs of Tennison comes during a scene of her in the incident

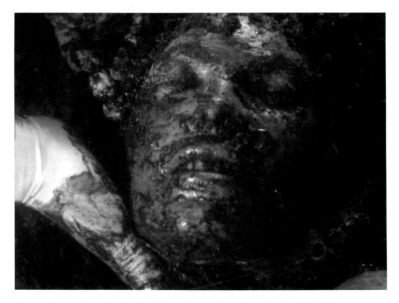

'I want to see her face': Tennison demands a closer look at Della's decomposing corpse

The consummate professional: Tennison eats lunch unperturbed by her surroundings

room reviewing the case. She stands alone in front of a wall of photos graphically picturing the victim's corpses, talking to the team while she casually eats a packet of crisps. The composition of the image marks both her affinity with and difference from the victims. While all of them, like Tennison, are lone women, any correspondence between them is unsettled by the uncomfortable juxtapositions of the shot, in which the decay and stillness of the pictures contrasts with Tennison's movement and drive to solve the case. As she eats, the sequence underlines how Tennison has a 'stomach' for this gut-wrenching work and this ability to remain emotionally distant from the bodies of the victims is one of the characteristics that most threatens to destabilise her perceived femininity. La Plante was insistent that Tennison should not be expected to react any differently to a male officer in the morgue, even when confronted with the bodies of other women.[58] But this is not to say by any means that she is left unaffected by her work.

Her partner Peter asks her after *Crime Night*, 'What about when you
see them in the morgue? Do you feel anything at all?' 'No' she replies.
'But you do feel'. In a rare moment of personal disclosure, she explains
that what she feels comes later, 'a pain' when she sees the parents and
family of the victim struggling to understand their loss: 'I feel it and I
hold on to it. Because it's up to me to find the man that destroyed that
life'.

It is important to note too, however, that the graphic
representation of the corpse is counterbalanced in some respects by
what we *don't* see. The audience is never witness to any of Marlow's
attacks, and never sees any of the women abducted, assaulted or
disposed of. In keeping with the wider traditions of the police
procedural, the actual execution of the crime itself is less important than
the detail of the investigation that follows. In this sense, much of *Prime
Suspect*'s early drama comes precisely in what is absent, in what it leaves
to the imagination. One of the first series' most haunting, horrifying
moments comes not in the morgue or with a shot of a victim's body, but
with the discovery of Marlow's lock-up. As Tennison and her team shine
their torches around the dank, dark cavernous space of the garage under
the railway arches the typically imperturbable Tennison emits a
horrified cry of 'Oh my God!' We look to see what she has seen – a set of
manacles fixed to a stained and bloodied wall, tracing the ghostly
imprint of the women's tortured bodies. As police and audience realise
this hellish place is where he 'strung them up', they must imagine for
themselves exactly what happened here. It is partly in this respect that
Prime Suspect 5 later fails to achieve the dramatic tension of the series'
best instalments. Not only is 'The Street' a jarringly overblown,
overplayed villain, the audience is made privy to scenes of his psychotic
ravings and the vicious slayings of his rivals. By opting to dramatise
some of these illicit deeds and the actual execution of his crimes, the plot
becomes increasingly convoluted and disparate and tension is
diminished rather than heightened. As a result, *Errors of Judgement* lost
the convincing procedural focus and suspense that the series delivered at
its most accomplished, amounting to an altogether unsatisfying

instalment that may in part account for the fact that seven years passed before *Prime Suspect 6: The Last Witness*.

A Genre in Transition

Over the decade and a half of *Prime Suspect*'s run, TV crime drama went through significant changes, some of them prompted by the series itself. Within this shifting landscape, *Prime Suspect* could not and did not remain static, so that the *Prime Suspect* of the 2000s was in many ways different to that of the early 1990s. With the simultaneous rise of 'docu-soap' and reality TV in this period, 'realism' was being newly inflected and contested in all sorts of ways across popular television. Within crime drama, the signifiers of realism had opened up to incorporate a 'glossier' look and more 'hi-tech' finish in many instances. Speaking to these changing aesthetics, *The Last Witness* (2003) drops the series' early use of a fly-on-the-wall documentary style to instead mount a thoroughly polished aesthetic, drawing on striking contemporary cinematographic effects. As Tennison struggles to trace Samira's final movements before her murder she interviews Stephen Abacha (Femi Oguns), an immigrant co-worker at the hotel where Samira worked twelve-hour shifts six days a week and the last person to see her alive. Abacha's boss can't tell Tennison where he is at first and they struggle to locate him in the soulless labyrinthine basement where he works. They eventually find him cleaning the men's urinals where he explains to Tennison that, like him, Samira was a 'ghost'; 'We don't exist', he tells her as she struggles to piece Samira's life together. It is this underground community's anxious, distorted perception of the city which particularly seems to be evoked by consistently filming the action through low angles and a fish-eye lens. This conspicuous effect frequently renders the urban environment acutely menacing. Spaces becomes misshapen, the image becomes warped and disconcerting as it curves perspective, and peripheral vision is lost as the corners of the frame fade into shadow.

87

Distorted spaces in *The Last Witness*: Tennison and Taff interview Stephen Abacha in the hotel basement where he works and in the tunnels by the London IMAX

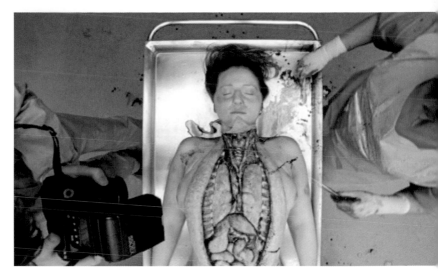

The spectacle of the corpse: Samira's torso lies graphically flayed open

Furthermore, if we compare the autopsy scene of *The Last* 89
Witness to that of the first *Prime Suspect*, more shifts in the aesthetics of
the series and, by extension, in the genre, become evident. Once again it
is a young woman who lies dead on the table. Here though, the first shot
of the body reveals how her entire torso has been flayed wide open by
the pathologist so that her internal organs are exposed in the chest
cavity, an image made even more arresting for being shot from above
with the camera poised directly over the body. This graphic display of
the interior body corresponds with shifts being spearheaded by *CSI* in
this period (and *Silent Witness* before that), in which forensic scenes
focus on the body's inner space, again seeking to make visible what had
not been seen before. In keeping with the fact that female professionals
had become more commonplace in crime drama, for the first time the
series features a woman pathologist, who pulls a scalpel from the body
as she explains 'The cartilages of the larynx are fractured'. Much of the
murder team sit watching the autopsy from behind a glass viewing
gallery, a new feature in the *mise en scène* of the morgue and one which

The autopsy as theatrical performance: Tennison's team watch proceedings from behind glass

foregrounds the sense of spectacle now commonly built into these scenes. The space of the autopsy room is illuminated by this reflective glass partition, the bright overhead lights and stainless steel surfaces, strikingly stylising proceedings and moving on from the seemingly more rudimentary morgue of the first series.

It is intriguing to note too that when Tennison arrives she foregoes the viewing gallery where the rest of the team sit, isolating herself from them to stand instead with the pathologist and get close to the body, remarking at the end 'She was beautiful'. The pathologist concurs, in a scene which might well be accused of indulging a distasteful voyeurism, seemingly suggesting that this case is more interesting, this victim more worthy of attention, and this lengthy post-mortem sequence more justifiable, *because* this is the body of a beautiful young woman. But Tennison's wish to get close to her speaks of more than this alone and rather of a desire to properly *see* the victim, unlike her colleagues who observe proceedings from behind a glass screen. At this late stage in her long career Tennison is still the maverick, insisting on working her cases her way; in this episode, for example, after learning her prime suspect, Milan Lukic (Oleg Men'shikov), is working for the British government and therefore 'immune' from prosecution, she risks violating the Official Secrets Act by arresting him nonetheless. Yet by this time she is also increasingly perceived as part of the 'old school' by her workmates, reluctantly edging (or rather being pressed) towards retirement. When she rejects the new practice of watching the autopsy from behind glass to attend the morgue in her own customary way, her distance from her younger colleagues and the new era of policing they belong to is brought home.

Interestingly, *The Last Witness* also contains perhaps the most anti-realist sequence of all the *Prime Suspect* series, the haunting scene where Tennison travels to Bosnia with her ex-partner, photojournalist Robert West (Liam Cunningham), to visit the location of the massacre her investigation has uncovered. One of the victims, Jasmina, has earlier described to Tennison how she and her sister were abducted from a bus by Serbian paramilitaries, held captive and raped, while all the men and boys with them were executed. There is no official record of the atrocity having occurred, but West manages to obtain a video from another journalist in which the local women are filmed discovering the men's bodies dumped in a disused warehouse. Tennison views the tape at West's home, but the audience does not get to see it with her. Rather it only hears the distressing soundtrack of the women's weeping and keening, and sees Tennison's pained reactions to the footage as the camera moves into a close-up of her horrified face watching events unfold.

After disobeying instructions not to travel to Bosnia to investigate the atrocity further, Tennison and West locate the abandoned hangar. Tennison walks inside and begins to look around her. In the stillness there now, shafts of light pour through the bullet holes that riddle the walls and birdsong fills the air, before she has what can only be described as a kind of 'flashback', a subjective vision of what happened there which vividly aligns us with her point of view. We see the dead bodies of the men piled up and the grief-stricken women coming inside and finding them, intercut with shots of Tennison's face

91

Tennison surveys the haunting scene of the massacre in Bosnia and 'remembers' the men's bodies piled up there

surveying her surroundings in the present as she 'remembers' what happened here. At no other point does the series play with temporality in this manner. As the sound of the women's wailing bleeds across the 'flashback' into the scenes of the warehouse now, past and present are interwoven. The scene is partly experienced as 'real' since it presents Tennison's memory of the video that was filmed there. Furthermore, both Tennison and the video footage are shot on hand-held camera, evoking all the realist connotations associated with this technique. But at the same time the scene is presented as if it is her subjective recollection (or perhaps imagining) of what happened. Dramatically, as we cut back and forth between the bereaved women and Tennison's face, the sequence is constructed as if she is *feeling* what happened here so that emotionally the audience experiences it from her perspective. Such a sequence would have been difficult to imagine in the first *Prime Suspect* and it demonstrates how elements of the series' style and address shifted as the scene moved through different writers and directors and through transitions in the crime-drama genre itself.

There was of course one element of the series that remained a constant throughout: Helen Mirren. La Plante has said of Mirren, 'I wanted her from day one'[59] and actress and role now seem impossible to extricate from one another. Even in the 1990s, when there was on-off speculation that *Prime Suspect* might be made into a film, the British press and series fans were incensed at rumours that Mirren might be replaced by a Hollywood star. Mirren's career has been marked by an impressive and often radical diversity, from being the young darling of the Royal Shakespeare Company at Stratford in the 1960s, to shocking cinema audiences with the X-rated *Caligula* (Tinto Brasi *et al.*, 1979), to seemingly entering the establishment with her Oscar-winning eponymous role in *The Queen* (Stephen Frears, 2006). But Tennison is the role which seems indelibly written into her star persona more than any other. In the next chapter I look more closely at what Mirren as an actor did with the role of Tennison and how this landmark character developed over the series' lifetime, before turning lastly to *The Final Act* and the debate that met it.

Conclusion: 'I got what I wanted. I got my job': Tennison Takes a Bow

By 2006 *Prime Suspect* had been an intermittent but eagerly awaited feature of British (and worldwide) television schedules for a decade and a half. This fact, combined with its predominant use of the miniseries/two x two-hour episode structure, enabled the programme to develop an unusually highly textured protagonist who grew and evolved as a character over a prolonged period of (real) time. Its miniseries format was not typical of TV crime drama, which tends towards the one-hour episodic and/or regular series format and is generally driven by the requirement to find the solution to a specific case each week. Certainly, when *Prime Suspect 4* experimented somewhat with its usual structure by switching to a three x two-hour self-contained episode format the result was a rather more formulaic outing with less complex characterisation than had previously been the case. *Inner Circles* in particular was the series' least memorable instalment, in which Tennison investigates the murder of a country-club manager and unravels a plot centring on local-council fraud. The move to vaguely suburban small-town England did not do well by Tennison or the framework of edgy, urban drama audiences had come to expect of the series, while the convoluted plotting made overall for a mediocre outing. *The Lost Child* and *The Scent of Darkness* at least worked as suspenseful thrillers, but the newly introduced time constraint meant they focused more heavily on the case in hand rather than interrogating the culture of contemporary policing, or Tennison herself, as the series did at its best.

By comparison, the more customarily unhurried structure of the other instalments enabled the series not merely to pursue intriguing red herrings and to tackle difficult and topical themes in a reflective fashion. The generous airtime given over to each episode also enabled a substantial degree of contemplative space for its (anti-)heroine to develop and for Mirren to refine a carefully nuanced performance over a number of years. In this chapter I look more closely at some of the detail of Mirren's persona and performance, which was central to how the series signalled its 'quality' status. Finally, I also reflect further on how Tennison evolved over the series' lifetime before examining the contentious series finale and its reception. Outside of soap opera, television drama has rarely followed a woman protagonist's development in this way or over such a period. By the time she finally and reluctantly confronted retirement in *The Final Act*, Tennison had fifteen years on the ambitious DCI first encountered in 1991. In this concluding episode, Tennison is visibly older, tangibly more vulnerable and painfully reviewing a career that has defined her life, as both she and the audience are compelled to reflect back on her experiences and the choices she has made. I argue that far from celebrating Tennison's career and achievements, the finale overwhelmingly positions her working life as one that has been marked by loss and sacrifice. Marginalising attention to what she has accomplished, it instead provides a melancholy exit for one of television drama's most memorable women. In the process, the finale whipped up a debate that demonstrated Tennison was perhaps always destined to go out on a wave of controversy; while a romantic happy-ever-after for Tennison would have been dismissed as an unlikely if convenient fantasy, the alternatives of killing her off or having her end up alone were inevitably going to be accused of sounding a dismal warning against the perils of being a career-driven woman.

Nothing Like a Dame: Being Jane Tennison

Mirren came to *Prime Suspect* with an impressive pedigree as a film and theatre actress and while she had appeared in a number of TV plays and series earlier in her career, it was nevertheless something of a *coup* for Granada to sign her up for the role of Tennison. After joining the Royal Shakespeare Company, in 1969 Mirren starred in the Michael Powell film, *Age of Consent*, playing a young girl who poses nude for a jaded elderly artist and becomes his muse. It was perhaps this role that clinched the 'sex queen' moniker that was to follow Mirren for the rest of her career, much to her chagrin. Yet, unusually, Mirren has managed to combine a reputation as an exceptional, 'serious' actress, with that of a slightly risqué one who holds no compunction about stripping off for a role when required. Celebrated for her performances in films including *The Long Good Friday* (John Mackenzie, 1980) and *Cal* (Pat O'Connor, 1984) she had also made forays into Hollywood, appearing in movies such as *White Nights* (Taylor Hackford, 1985) and *The Mosquito Coast* (Peter Weir, 1986). Despite this, she was not widely known in the US when *Prime Suspect* was made, a state of affairs the series would quickly alter. The show kick-started Mirren's career in the US, something that her film projects prior to this time had signally failed to do, bringing her national acclaim on Masterpiece Theatre along with several Emmy awards and nominations.[60] In 2007 Mirren's rise to international recognition reached a new peak when she won the Academy Award for Best Actress for *The Queen*, shortly after *Prime Suspect: The Final Act* was broadcast. In fact, *The Final Act* appears to make a playful nod to her having just completed this role when half-smiling she reprises her signature line to DS Simms (Robert Pugh), telling him in a knowing, tongue-in-cheek fashion, 'Don't call me ma'am, I'm not the bloody Queen!'

The casting of Mirren in *Prime Suspect* brought with it some interesting expectations and nuances. The above-the-title status of her name in the opening credits underlined both the fact of her star power in Britain and that her presence was indicative of the programme's aspirations to quality status, as if this alone differentiated it from the everyday mass of TV cop shows. Equally, her performance won column inches because of the perception that it required her to play 'against type'. The role of a steely, forty-ish detective working round the clock to save her career and lock up a serial killer seemingly offered little opportunity for racy interludes. However, Mirren's persona and past performances brought an extra edge to those scenes where male colleagues speculate crudely about her desirability, and to the reception of the series, as critics pondered this 'sex queen's' ageing appearance. As Tennison she would bare every wrinkle and frown line to the scrutiny of the camera, no small order in an industry obsessed with the youthfulness of its women stars. She would win many plaudits for her willingness to do so, proving in the role that women 'of a certain age' could carry a major TV drama.

Mirren's performance throughout *Prime Suspect* was richly understated, particularly given her background as an actress in the theatre, with its more demonstrative acting style. It is instead marked by its small, controlled gestures, which perfectly capture Tennison's awareness that she is under the constant surveillance of rivals willing her to fail. Mirren has described how she realised that she must closely monitor her body language to play Tennison convincingly after meeting with 'the woman in charge of Holloway police station'. This officer was to give her some indispensable insights:

> She gave me the most valuable advice: never let them see you cry, and never cross your arms. When I asked why, she said, 'Because it is a defensive action and therefore weak'. The police are masters when it comes to body language. She went on to tell me that, if you want to show power over someone, you should touch him or her lightly on the arm … . Throughout *Prime Suspect* I don't think I ever crossed my arms, and Jane Tennison only cries in private.[61]

Nowhere is Mirren's understated performance technique more apparent or better utilised by the series than in the close-up. If all the instalments

97

of *Prime Suspect* have any aesthetic motif in common, employed by each of the directors who took the helm over the series' duration, it is in the constant, contemplative return to Tennison's/Mirren's face. It is partly because film and television possess the facility to employ the close-up that they are inescapably qualitatively different to theatre. Cinema realised the power of the close-up relatively early in its history, both as a means to communicate important plot information and to make icons of its stars. But it could be argued that television, more than any other, is the medium of the close-up. It is through the close-up that television uses the small space of the screen to its full potential, bringing faces and emotions into the intimacy of the audience's homes in the most affecting manner possible.

In the first *Prime Suspect* the 'gendering' of the camerawork is evident not just in the way it frames Tennison in isolation away from the mass of men on her team, but also in the way that she is recurrently distinguished by a motionless camera, often lingering on her in close-up after or outside the dramatic climax of a scene. Here the series uses a convention particularly associated with soap opera and its visual tradition of staying with a close-up of the protagonist's face for that 'extra beat' beyond the palpable end of a scene. In the hallway outside the incident room after she first addresses the men on her team, and again after DI Burkin ejects her from the room where she has insensitively questioned the grief-stricken Major Howard, we do not cut to the next scene immediately or witness the more tangible drama of the men's reactions to her. Instead, we stay with Tennison and are invited to read the subtle, indeterminate shifts on her face: relief at having delivered her first briefing to a hostile audience without faltering; remorse at having badgered a victim's parent; and later, vindication at having secured a confession. The ambivalent characterisation of Tennison, and Mirren's reserved performance style, meant that much of how the audience perceives Tennison comes from the readings we make of her in these instants. They constitute moments of reflective intimacy with the viewer that other characters are not privy to, pauses which encourage a greater will to understand or identify with her. Such moments were all the more important to audience empathy since on La Plante's early advice at the start of filming, Mirren consciously avoided smiling in the role. 'It's a very female thing, ... [to] smile, because you want to charm people and manipulate them through charm' she has observed, but as La Plante explained, '[Tennison] doesn't work that way'.[62]

The extent to which the programme should explore Tennison as an individual and dramatise her personal life, as opposed to focusing on her investigations, soon became the subject of some debate among both the production team and audiences. While La Plante had parted company with the programme partly because she felt pressured to write more about Tennison's private life, Mirren was in favour of cultivating this aspect of Tennison, enthusing in interview that, 'I love it that the audience have embraced this character and written in to say they want to see the personal side of her'.[63] In recognition of Mirren's growing star power and bankability, as the series went on she had increasingly come to command influence on its production and direction. Hence, she also apparently drove the decisions not only to introduce the self-contained two-hour format to *Prime Suspect 4*,[64] but to relocate the setting of *Prime Suspect 5: Errors of Judgement* from London to Manchester[65] and to focus extensively on Tennison's increasingly lonely and fragile personal life in *The Final Act*.[66] Looking back at her achievements on the series she has even commented, 'As an actor what I've enjoyed the most is to be able to be proactive in the whole process, in the scripts, in the choice of directors, in the choice of writers and to know that my voice is heard'.[67]

However, while later instalments of the programme had continued to command big audiences and win awards, they did not all deliver the dramatic finesse of the original series. There was a sense in some quarters after *Prime Suspect 5* that the series had passed its peak. While Mirren had apparently welcomed audience interest in Tennison's private life, evidently not everyone felt the same way, with one reviewer disparagingly commenting after her misjudged affair in *Prime Suspect 5* that, 'We look at Jane Tennison now ... and despite Helen Mirren's durable panache reluctantly conclude that she did become a bit of an old boot with an appetite for juicy young policemen'.[68] Here the writer's objection seems to be not merely to the fact that a cop show should digress into romantic territory, but that an older woman (even a 'durable' one) should be portrayed as sexually active. His comments underline again how women protagonists 'of a certain age', especially single ones, continue to constitute a problem which unsettles and perplexes television, or its male critics at least. Perhaps sensing that the programme had passed its best, and keen to avoid being typecast or too closely associated with a single character, Mirren declared this would be her last outing as Tennison.

Seven years later, though, she was enticed back and once more declared that this would be the end of the series. *The Last Witness* again sought to give screentime to Tennison's personal life, but did so in a rather more nuanced and absorbing fashion than some of the earlier series. There is again a passing love interest as she briefly rekindles her relationship with Robert West, whom we gather from brief allusions to their past had been her partner at some point in the years since the last series. More interesting, though, is the manner in which the series revisits her relationship with her family, specifically her father. As she visits him in his austere and starkly lit retirement home, we surmise also that in the intervening years he has entered residential care and that her absent mother has died. It is the first real scene with her family since the original *Prime Suspect*, where she was last seen bawling her father out on his birthday for failing to video her appearance on *Crime Night*.

Not much appears to have changed in her priorities since this time, as he observes when she arrives that 'I hope you're going to stay long enough to take your coat off'. He counsels her to take the retirement option she is being encouraged to consider, telling her it's 'Time you got out of the sewers'. Naturally Tennison chooses not to take his advice and there is a touching awkwardness visible between them as she momentarily hesitates to take his hand when they talk. But this episode also reinstates the relationship with her father as being a pivotal one for Tennison, one she takes comfort from when she must face a moral dilemma alone. During her investigation she learns that Milan Lukic is being shielded from prosecution for war crimes by the British

Father (Frank Finlay) and daughter share a tender moment

government. She realises that to go after him would be to directly
contravene orders and jeopardise investigations being pursued under the
protection of the Official Secrets Act. Momentarily ceasing to be a
prominent senior cop, and instead becoming a daughter who is lost and
needs guidance, it is her father to whom she turns for advice, confiding
in him simply 'I don't know what to do'. He reassures her that she will
do the right thing, but it is a scene which reminds us of how acutely
alone Tennison is. Throughout the series' lifetime, lovers and partners
consistently depart or disappoint, and while Haskons and Taff look out
for her well-being she is never allowed a single friend to call her own.
The brief return to her family in this episode reminds us of the weight of
her isolation and the vulnerability that comes with it.

101

How Do You Solve a Problem Like Tennison?: *The Final Act*

Perhaps because of the return to form achieved by *Prime Suspect 6: The Last Witness*, and as ITV sought to return to some of its past glories by reviving both *Prime Suspect* and *Cracker* (1993–), Mirren agreed to reprise the role one more time in *The Final Act*. As the series reached its end it explicitly sought not merely to provide Tennison with one last intriguing case but to revisit and confront her personal demons, exploring her estrangement from her family, her increasing isolation and dependency on alcohol and even her fraught history with Bill Otley. Tennison's private life here finally becomes at least as important as the investigation – the murder of a teenage girl – weighted though this is with the significance of its being her last case.

Tennison had always unwound with a drink after a difficult day, just like generations of hardened cops before her, and her growing reliance on booze had been hinted at before now. But the immediacy and extent of her decline into full-blown alcoholism in *The Final Act* still come as a jolt, especially as this is not particularly signalled in *The Last Witness*. As the drama opens she is seen waking up on the sofa, looking dishevelled and worn out in the cold morning light. A whisky bottle on the table confirms that this is a hangover while bleak, foreboding music

Tennison wakes up in an alcoholic haze at the start of *The Final Act*

connotes that she is in the midst of dark times. Looking at her watch, she swears as she realises she's overslept and looks confusedly at the phone next to her lying off the hook. Later at the office it will emerge that Tennison had taken an important call the night before about the missing teenager, Sallie Sturdy (Maxine Barton), but she has no recollection of it. Soon enough Sallie's dead body will be found on the local heath and her murder will constitute Tennison's last case. Now, as Tennison wakes and tries to piece together the previous evening, her bewilderment is intercut with scenes of the missing girl's mother running through the streets frantically looking for her daughter. Tennison looks in the mirror, perplexed to find a bruise on her head, then notices that oddly the toilet seat in the bathroom has been left up. Going to her bedroom, she pulls back her duvet and stands looking at her bed, as we and she start to surmise that she may well have had a one-night stand she can't remember.

Alarm bells ring loudly in this startling opening sequence and not merely because last night's binge-drinking (and indeed years of bad habits) have left her looking so suddenly and terribly aged. Rather, what is equally disconcerting in these early scenes is how Tennison's professionalism has apparently deserted her. Her drinking has caused a blackout so encompassing that she can't remember the Sallie Sturdy case being called in, and her hangover has made her late for work, lapses the Tennison of old would not have tolerated. On the eve of her retirement, drinking for Tennison now signifies vulnerability and weakness, not toughness and attitude. Taff is horrified when she admits to him that she can't remember leaving the pub the night before, exclaiming 'Jesus, Jane! You've got to look after yourself. What's the matter with you?' Her risk-taking connotes not the figure of the maverick cop but disorder, a loose cannon who can't be relied upon.

Later, her boss DCS Mitchell (Brendan Coyle) is appalled when she conducts an interview with Sallie's grieving father while smelling of alcohol, and she only narrowly avoids spending her final weeks on compulsory sick leave. He reminds her that she has been advised before to go to addiction counselling and she is shamed into resuming

103

Otley wins redemption, befriending Tennison before sacrificing his own life to help her

attendance at Alcoholics Anonymous following this dressing-down. There she unexpectedly meets Bill Otley, now a changed man and reformed alcoholic. Winning her forgiveness and earning redemption, he apologises unreservedly for the treacherous way he treated her years earlier, becoming her unlikely confidant as her world increasingly begins to crumble. Mitchell tries to offer her support as she stubbornly refuses to retire a moment before she has to, but for him Tennison has become a liability, part of the dated culture she once took a stand against; 'Old school, that's Tennison. On the force, what, thirty, thirty-five years? Battered, burnt out. Dinosaurs. And what do they do when they leave? They drink themselves to death, that's what'. Reduced to knocking back straight vodka for breakfast before driving to the office, the once poised, unflappable, unswerving Tennison has become unrecognisable.

For all its polish and tension, *The Final Act* makes for difficult viewing, as it chips away at Tennison's dignity and ability to do the job she loves. Her once trusted instinct seems lost to her as she misses clues, lets her suspect Curtis Flynn (Heshima Thompson) slip through her fingers and fails to see till the last juncture that Sallie's killer, her classmate Penny (Laura Greenwood), was there in front of her all along.

As the case progresses, the two strike up a friendship and Tennison can't help falling for this bright, spirited girl who reminds her of herself as she once was. But she is struck another blow when she learns that her father is dying. She insists on getting a second opinion, a gesture which speaks of her shame at having neglected him for so long, and of denial that it's too late to make amends, rather than any real likelihood of his recovery. In a series of deeply touching scenes, father and daughter reconcile at the hospital after he tells her that she has to accept he is dying and makes it clear that he doesn't resent her actions: 'You pursued your career, you followed your life. That meant you had less to do with other people. You feel bad about that, but why should you? It was what you had to do'. Later she cries at his bedside as he sleeps, telling him 'I love you, Dad, I've always loved you. Even when I was too busy and I didn't see you'. When he dies later that night, Otley is the only person she can think to call.

True to form, though, she is late for the funeral and then interrupts the ceremony when her mobile phone rings. In the pub afterwards with her sister and niece she gets drunk and abusive, estranging them once and for all. Her sister Pauline (Carolyn Pickles)

'I've always loved you': Tennison prepares for her father's death at his hospital bedside

On a wave of nostalgia, Tennison dons her old police cap

walks out, telling her 'I'm sorry it's turned out like this. I hope you got what you wanted from life, I really do. I hope it was worth it'. Her use of the past tense seems significant, as if to say Tennison's life is already over, underlining the sense of nostalgia and melancholy that permeates the finale. As Tennison visits her parents' home, drunkenly dons her old WPC cap and dances alone in her bedroom to the faded LPs of her youth, she cuts a tragic figure. What would her teenaged self, who first put on a police cap when she was just seventeen years old, make of the woman she has become? In *Prime Suspect 3* Tennison expresses no regrets to Jake that she didn't choose a life and family with him over her career all those years ago, observing 'I got what I wanted. I got my job'. Later, in *Prime Suspect 5* Ballinger tells her that DI Devanney specifically asked to work under her when she relocated to Manchester, telling her 'You're a role model Jane, an icon in the force'. Yet *The Final Act* does little to celebrate Tennison's life and career or to recall what she achieved. Instead it is preoccupied with ghosts from the past, lost hopes, unfulfilled possibilities.

It is deeply telling that Tennison's last case sees her investigating the murder of a teenage girl and befriending another in the process, reminding us again of her own 'lost child'. Tennison shows more fondness for Penny and is more candid with her than with anyone we have ever seen her with. In one exchange, she takes her to a gallery to see a picture she had loved as a girl, Joshua Reynolds's portrait of 'The Strawberry Girl'. The scene brings with it new insight into Tennison, as we learn she had once been passionate about art, and we witness a moment of unusual sentimentality in her wish to share the picture with Penny. After Sallie's funeral, Tennison confides in Penny that her father is dying and Penny remarks, 'You don't seem sad. You seem lonely'. Finally, Tennison admits to her, and to herself, 'Yeah, I am. I am lonely'. Penny stands symbolically both for Tennison's own lost youth, that moment of teenage promise when the world was still hers for the taking, and for the child she never had. It is not so much that she manipulates Tennison as fulfils a need in her. So completely does she win Tennison's affection that she blinds her to the truth of the case, compromising her professional distance and objectivity. 'She stole my heart', Tennison admits helplessly to DI Traynor (Robbie Gee). 'Who'd have thought?'

Ultimately Tennison solves the case, as she swore she would, but it costs her dearly to do so. By the end of *The Final Act*, the two

Another 'lost child': Tennison and Penny comfort each other after Sallie's funeral

107

figures who'd offered some hope that she wouldn't be left entirely alone at the end are taken from her, Otley gunned down by Curtis Flynn in a car park for trying to help her, Penny locked away. Otley thus departs the series endowed with heroic status, but no such honour is bestowed on Tennison. In contrast to the ending of the first *Prime Suspect*, which saw her crack the case and jubilantly celebrate with her team, Tennison leaves the office here for the final time on her own, so estranged from everyone that she chooses not to go to her own retirement party. For all these reasons, *The Final Act* proved highly divisive among audiences and critics, giving rise to some animated debate. Had this bleak ending simply remained true to the programme's original realist, 'gritty' aspirations? Or had the series instead betrayed the conviction of the early Jane Tennison for a sadly reactionary and all-too-predictable portrayal of her demise – a dire lesson for women everywhere reminding them that the price to be paid for devoting oneself so single-mindedly to one's work is loneliness?

Just a Cop-out?: Saying Farewell to Tennison

The problem of how to end *Prime Suspect* satisfactorily was signalled before the finale even came to the screen, by what appears to have been a troubled production background. In the run-up to the show, the media had speculated about Tennison's fate, focusing on the suggestion that she would be killed off one way or another. But in an 'exclusive' *Daily Telegraph* interview following its broadcast, executive producer Andy Harries revealed how Mirren had objected to this. She wanted instead 'to leave her character with the possibility of redemption through Alcoholics Anonymous' and for the final episodes 'to focus on a personal journey for Det Supt Tennison ... it was this requirement that caused the writers so much difficulty'.[69] In fact such was the 'difficulty' that the original writer, Peter Berry, who'd penned the intelligent and atmospheric *Prime Suspect 6*, was replaced by a new one, Frank Deasy, in September 2005. This left relatively little time to deliver a final script before shooting began in March 2006. Harries had considered having Tennison battle cancer in the finale, but eventually Berry had written her out as a prescription-pill addict. In Harries's words though, 'It didn't feel quite right. The drink felt much better – she'd always been a drinker', prompting the crucial narrative shift subsequently incorporated by Deasy. Where all parties were agreed at least, was that Tennison should not end up in a relationship and so 'the possibility of romance was quickly ruled out'.[70]

What is striking about this account of the scriptwriting process is the manner in which it reveals the presumption that Tennison had to bow out alone and afflicted, be that through illness or addiction. Hope for 'redemption' or recovery might be allowed, but contentment certainly was not. Was this again merely in keeping with the generic tradition of the devoted lone detective? The *Independent on Sunday* evidently thought so, with Hermione Eyre clearly having found it all rather derivative, asking 'Why is it that all detectives over time come to resemble Raymond Chandler's Philip Marlowe? ... [Tennison] spent most of last week's final double bill driving through the rain (Marlowe never goes out without his personal rain machine) and waking up not quite sure where she was, or why, but certain it wasn't good'.[71] Or was this ending evidence of misogynistic tunnel vision, a consequence of having a predominantly male team of writers and producers overseeing Tennison's demise? Fifteen years after audiences and critics first found themselves debating whether La Plante had let the feminist side down by refusing to allow Tennison to both catch her man (Marlow) and keep her man (Peter), the same arguments were rolled out and rehearsed again; why did Tennison have to be punished for her professional success at the cost of her personal happiness? Alternatively, would it have been spurious and naive to pretend that women were really any closer now to 'having it all' than they were in 1991?

Indicating some of the conflicting responses that *The Final Act* provoked, the London *Metro* reviewer heaped praise on the finale. Observing that 'it takes a lot for a show to so grip and absorb me that I can't leave the telly', the writer reflected that that this was an emotional

109

'character study far more than a crime thriller', where 'the extreme bleakness ... drew you still closer to the prickly Tennison'.[72] In contrast, for Libby Brooks, writing in the *Guardian*, it was a deeply demoralising experience:

> Vodka for breakfast, poisoned relationships and an empty future: the final episode of *Prime Suspect* offered a dismal portrayal of the older woman who had concentrated on her career ... it was a depressing ending for a character who was emblematic of women's struggle to succeed in the workplace.[73]

Brooks's review led to some heated exchanges between readers on the Guardian Unlimited web forum, debating the relative merits of the ending and whether Tennison's alcoholism signalled anything more than a generic convention. Some posters thought the ending entirely appropriate, realistically sombre and even positive in some respects.[74] Others objected to Brooks's suggestion that the ending punished Tennison for being an overambitious woman, with one asking,

110

> Why should a female detective character have to have an upbeat ending just because she's female? Crime dramas routinely portray major characters who are grievously damaged by the grimness of the job they do ... . It's a convention of the genre, nothing more and nothing less.[75]

In a similar vein, some viewers noted that Tennison was not alone in her decline in the finale, since Otley was similarly seen to have ended up damaged and alone with a drink problem. But not all participants bought this argument and its effacement of the significance of gender, instead faulting 'a bunch of male writers giving vent to their undoubtedly bigoted, sexist and prejudiced opinions about women in power positions'.[76] As 'Bjerkley' astutely summed it up:

> Case of the Murder of the Idea of Equality: Solved
> Culprit: Male scriptwriter
> Weapon: Pen

Place: In every TV room in the country
Motive: Keeping ITV viewers/*Daily Mail* readers happy, popularizing the
message "You can't have it all".

(Grieving mother, Lynda La Plante, has been notified).[77]

The debate took another high-profile twist when La Plante herself
became embroiled in discussion of the series end and whether it had been
a mistake to have Tennison finish up an alcoholic. La Plante has openly
admitted she stopped watching *Prime Suspect* after the fourth miniseries,
following her differences with Granada. She had also apparently had a
difference of opinion with Helen Mirren when she was approached to
write *Prime Suspect* 6 and Mirren vetoed her ideas about the future of the
character.[78] Appearing on BBC *Breakfast* (2000–) to publicise her latest
book three days before the finale was to go out, La Plante was asked
about her feelings regarding the series' ending. Breaking her customarily
rather noncommittal response to questions about the later series, she
criticised the storyline, saying 'I find it very sad that for the end of a great
character, female, somebody has to say "Make her a drunk"'.[79]

La Plante's frustration and disappointment were clearly
mirrored by that of many fans. But ultimately the writers of *The Final
Act* were caught between a rock and a hard place, so great was the
challenge of finding a suitable ending for Tennison. Were they to have
Tennison retire contentedly into the arms of her lover and family,
vindicated for her choices and celebrated by all, they would stand
accused of peddling fantasy; were they to have her finish lonely and
broken, they would stand accused of denying single, professional
women the prospect of personal happiness. Like the closing scenes of
previous instalments, the final images of Tennison, which show her
missing her own party to instead walk out of the office alone and
disappear into the anonymity of London's streets, carry a certain air of
open-endedness. She walks with poise and a faint smile, but there is an
ambiguity to these last moments which echoes a realist tradition in film,
posing the questions, where will she go now, what will she do, what

Case closed: Tennison solves Sallie's murder and walks away into retirement

112   does her future hold? Refusing sentimentality, *The Final Act* offers no
trite or comforting answers to these uncertainties.

Over But Not Out: Tennison's Legacy

To conclude finally, though, I want to reflect not on the irresolvable
conflicts embodied by Tennison but instead to consider the bequest she
made within, and even beyond, the margins of the small screen. For it
would be reductive to suggest that *The Final Act* alone constitutes how
she will be remembered. What remained indisputable in the debates that
followed the last episode was the impact of *Prime Suspect* on TV crime
drama, heralding as it did the start of a tremendous period of
international growth and expansion for the genre. As has been explored,
the cop show went through a period of marked regeneration following
the success of La Plante's creation. Women police are now a widespread
presence on our screens, and not merely in the roles of assistant or

sidekick to a male superior. Rather, the skilful, serious, senior female investigator who seemed such a novelty in 1991 is now in evidence across crime drama. From DCI Janine Lewis (Caroline Quentin) in *Blue Murder* (ITV, 2003–) to Deputy Police Chief Brenda Johnson (Kyra Sedgwick) in *The Closer* (TNT, 2005–) women are now far more frequently cast as the lead protagonist in cop shows. So too, as we have seen, has the genre frequently come to place forensic detail at its centre as a marker of its authenticity. This shift is one that might also be linked to the simultaneous rise of fly-on-the-wall police documentaries and real-crime TV since the 1990s, expanding audiences' appetite for such scientific and technical matter (a fact which begs the question, did the growth of crime drama fuel the taste for real-crime TV, or vice versa?). While historical, period-set and more traditional 'classic' television detectives still hold an enduring appeal for audiences, their contemporaries are now often to be found contemplating the finer points of blood-splatter analysis, bullet striations or DNA breakdowns. Again, within this shift women have been widely featured as adept at forensic work. This is evident not merely in the *Crime Scene Investigation* franchise (cf. Sara Sidle [Jorja Fox] in the original *CSI* or Dr Alexx Woods [Khandi Alexander] in *CSI: Miami* [2002–]) but also in series such as *Waking the Dead* and *Crossing Jordan* (NBC, 2001–7). More recently, in September 2009 *Prime Suspect*'s continuing resonance was made evident once again when NBC announced that the channel plans to remake the 'iconic title' in the US.[80]

113

Of course we should be wary of simply presuming that the greater visibility of women in TV crime drama equates to 'progress' in the representation of women, as previously seen in regard to debates about *Juliet Bravo*. American crime series in particular maintain a fondness for using their female cops and forensics experts to bring a touch of lip-glossed glamour to proceedings. In addition, a feminist critique of the rise of women within TV forensics in particular might argue that this branch of police work merely positions them as rightfully belonging 'inside', working in the lab or morgue, rather than 'outside' in the public world where men are active. Yet it is still undeniable that the quantity and diversity of women's roles in crime drama is greater now than it has ever been. Furthermore, some reports have suggested that women viewers have taken inspiration from these female characters as role models, motivating them to pursue careers in crime investigation, particularly in forensic science.[81] *Prime Suspect* did not itself focus on a woman forensics expert. But what it did do was construct a woman character at ease in the world of forensics, one who sought to understand the dead body and all its secrets, knowing this could be central to solving the crime, and for this alone the figure of Tennison was a precursor of these changing roles for women, both on and off screen.

For La Plante, the suggestion that *Prime Suspect* may have played even a minor part in opening up women's sense of their career options, or expanding the viewing public's impression of what constitutes proper 'female' work, would vindicate the series' achievements more than any award could.[82] It is a legacy, too, that one imagines Tennison would have been proud of, a fitting tribute to the job she loved even in the midst of the many professional battles she endured. In this respect, the Tennison we might best remember is the one in *Prime Suspect 5* who has to address a group of uninterested schoolkids in a deprived area of Manchester. She has prepared a speech but she reads it only halfheartedly and realises she is failing to capture their imagination. Putting her notes aside she looks at them and it seems for a moment that she sees the reality of their lives and lack of choices and wants more than anything for them to escape this, to have ambition and to fulfil it, as she has. 'I've been a cop for about twenty-two years', she tells them. 'When I was about your age I decided what I wanted. I wanted to be in the police force. And that's where I am. And I'm very happy about that'.

Notes

1 Elaine Paterson, 'Gritty Woman', *Time Out*, 10 April 1991, p. 136.

2 Philip Purser, 'Prejudice? It's a Fair Cop', *Daily Telegraph*, 10 April 1991, p. 14.

3 In this book I will situate *Prime Suspect* as both a 'cop show' and more broadly a 'crime drama', using the latter as an umbrella term which encompasses various crime-themed subgenres, from series about uniformed police or plain-clothes detectives, to forensics and law-enforcement employees undertaking investigative work, to private investigators and amateur sleuths.

4 Paterson, 'Gritty Woman', p. 136.

5 It could be argued in fact that these 'forensic detective' roles merely extend existing traditional cultural associations which twin femininity with the 'abject' body.

6 Amy Taubin, 'Misogyny, She Wrote', *Village Voice*, 28 January 1992, p. 50.

7 With the exception of *Prime Suspect 4*, which consisted of three separate two-hour stories, all the *Prime Suspects* were originally broadcast in the UK in a two part x two-hour 'miniseries' format. Full details and dates can be found in the Credits at the end of this volume.

8 She also provided the storyline for *Prime Suspect 2* and as a crime novelist wrote books of the first three miniseries.

9 See for example Julia Hallam, *Lynda La Plante* (Manchester: Manchester University Press, 2005), p. 100. La Plante's account here seems somewhat surprising given the amount of time she subsequently dedicated to the (highly melodramatic) private life of her police-woman heroine Clare Blake (Amanda Burton) in *The Commander* (ITV, 2003). When I asked La Plante in interview at the 2007 Crime Wave season how she would have developed Tennison had she continued writing the series, she replied that after she and *Prime Suspect* parted ways she developed *The Commander* from the 'storyline that I wanted to write for Helen [Mirren] ... because I felt that Jane Tennison was such a character and such an icon for women ... that she would be incredible material to be a Commander within the police force'. Yet ironically much of the first part of *The Commander* focuses not on Blake's work but on her unlikely romantic relationship with a convicted murderer. (Lynda La Plante in interview with Natasha Cooper at the Brixton Ritzy for the BFI Crime Wave season, 9 September 2007).

10 Cited in Anthony Hayward and Amy Rennert (eds), *Prime Suspect: The Official Book of the Award-Winning Series* (London: Carlton Books, 1996), p. 14.

11 Hallam, *Lynda La Plante*, p. 11.

12 Ibid., pp. 33–4.

13 Ibid., p. 35. As Hallam also notes (and as the Credits at the end of this book underline), in a seemingly regressive shift, by the time of *Prime Suspect 6* there were 'no longer any women involved in the key creative and/or institutional positions' in the series (p. 102 n1).

14 Lynda La Plante in interview with Natasha Cooper.

15 Ibid.

16 See for example Purser, 'Prejudice?', p. 14.

17 Lynda La Plante in interview with Natasha Cooper.

18 Purser, 'Prejudice?', p. 14.

19 Angela Lambert, 'DCI Jane Tennison? Yes, That Was Me', *Independent*, 15 June 1993, p. 18.

20 Charlotte Brunsdon, 'Men's Genres for Women', in Helen Baehr and Gillian Dyer (eds), *Boxed In: Women and Television* (London: Pandora, 1987), p. 193.

21 Ibid.

22 Ellis Cashmore, … *and there was television* (New York and London: Routledge, 1994), p. 155.

23 Ibid.

24 In October 1985 PC Keith Blakelock was killed during riots at the Broadwater Farm Estate in Tottenham, London. The disturbances were prompted by the death of a local black woman during a police raid at her home.

25 My necessarily brief overview of this canon does not have sufficient space to challenge the premises underlying it or develop it by exploring 'missing' programmes. But it remains important to reflect on *why* it is certain programmes have made it to the canon where others failed. From the availability of archive recordings, to the 'star power' of charismatic performers, to the perceived capacity of a programme to speak to the topical concerns of its times, numerous factors inform why given shows have come to constitute the chronicles of TV crime drama and to exemplify the shifts therein.

26 Robert Reiner, 'The Dialectics of Dixon: The Changing Image of the TV Cop', in Mike Stephens and Saul Becker (eds), *Police Force, Police Service: Care and Control in Britain* (Basingstoke: Macmillan, 1994), pp. 11–32.

27 Reiner, 'The Dialectics of Dixon', p. 11.

28 Charlotte Brunsdon, 'Structure of Anxiety: Recent British Television Crime Fiction', *Screen* vol. 39 no. 3, Autumn 1998, p. 223.

29 Brunsdon, 'Men's Genres for Women', pp. 184–5.

30 Ibid., p. 19.

31 No doubt partly on the back of the success of *The Silence of the Lambs*, there was speculation for some time after the series was broadcast that *Prime Suspect* would be remade as a Hollywood film, but the project never materialised.

32 Linda Mizejewski, *Hardboiled and High Heeled* (London and New York: Routledge, 2004), pp. 60–1.

33 Ibid.

34 Gillian Dyer, 'Women and Television: An Overview', in Helen Baehr and Gillian Dyer (eds) *Boxed In: Women and Television* (London: Pandora, 1987), p. 11.

35 See <http://news.bbc.co.uk/onthisday>.

36 Dyer, 'Women and Television', pp. 10–11.

37 Julie D'Acci, 'The Case of Cagney and Lacey', in Baehr and Dyer, *Boxed In*, p. 206.

38 Ibid., p. 223.

39 *Prime Suspect: Behind the Scenes*, DVD Extra in the *Prime Suspect Complete Collection*, Granada Ventures (ITV DVD) Ltd (2006).

40 Glen Creeber, 'Cigarettes and Alcohol: Investigating Gender, Genre and Gratification in *Prime Suspect*', *Television and New Media* vol. 2 no. 2 (2001), p. 162.

41 Much of the episode similarly plays without a music soundtrack, but at certain moments, such as the discovery of the body at Sunningdale, a haunting, neoclassical composition is drawn on to heighten emotionality. Written by the accomplished, Academy Award-winning film and TV composer Steven Warbeck, the score punctuates the drama subtly in an effective, sometimes discordant manner, earning him a Best Original TV Music BAFTA nomination. The contribution his music made to the temperament of the programme is underlined by the fact that he went on to compose the music for the first five of the *Prime Suspect* miniseries. In contrast to Warbeck's style, the sinister, foreboding music of *The Final Act* in particular is used insistently throughout, becoming intrusive at times.

42 Anon., review of *Prime Suspect*, *Sunday Times*, 14 April 1991, np.

43 Peter Paterson, 'A Plain Jane to Rush Home To', *Daily Mail*, 9 April 1991, p. 24.

44 Paterson, 'Gritty Woman', p. 136.

45 Broadcasting Standards Council, finding from BSC Complaints Committee, 28 May 1991.

46 Greeber, 'Cigarettes and Alcohol', p. 152.

47 *Prime Suspect: Behind the Scenes*, DVD Extra in the *Prime Suspect Complete Collection*, Granada Ventures (ITV DVD) Ltd (2006).

48 Black teenager Stephen Lawrence was murdered in a racist attack in South East London in 1993. The case attracted massive media coverage as police failed to bring successful charges against the five prime suspects. Outrage at this outcome led to a public inquiry, headed by Sir William Macpherson and a report, published in 1999, which found that 'institutional racism' was pervasive in the Metropolitan Police.

49 Hallam, *Lynda La Plante*, p. 82.

50 Ibid., p. 83.

51 Purser, 'Prejudice?', p. 14.

52 Joan Smith, *Misogynies* (revised edition, 1993, first published 1989) (London: Faber and Faber, 1993), pp.169–70. 'Jack the Ripper' infamously mutilated and murdered at least five women working as prostitutes in the Whitechapel area of East London in 1888.

53 Interestingly Mirren also appeared in the British 1993 film inspired by the Ripper case, *The Hawk* (dir David Hayman). In a role far removed from Tennison, she plays Annie Marsh, a Manchester housewife who increasingly comes to suspect that her travelling-salesman husband may be a serial killer.

54 Smith, *Misogynies*, p. 175.

55 Frances Gibb, 'The DNA Scientist Who Made Individuals of Us All', *The Times* online, 6 December 2006, available at <www.timesonline.co.uk/tol/life_and_style/career_and_jobs/legal/article745719.ece>, accessed 1 April 2008.

56 Jessica Rogers, 'A Life of Crime', *Broadcast*, 30 November 2007, p. 25.

57 Richard Last, 'Murder and Male Prejudice', *Daily Telegraph*, 8 April 1991, p. 15.

58 In conversation with Natasha Cooper.

59 Ibid.

60 Mirren won the 1996 'Outstanding Lead Actress in a Miniseries or Special' Emmy for *Prime Suspect: The Scent of Darkness* and the 2007 'Outstanding Lead Actress in a Miniseries or Movie' Emmy for *Prime Suspect: The Final Act*, as well as being nominated on four other occasions for *Prime Suspect 2*; *Prime Suspect 3*; *Prime Suspect 5: Errors of Judgement* and *Prime Suspect 6: The Last Witness*.

61 Helen Mirren, *In the Frame: My Life in Words and Pictures* (London: Weidenfeld and Nicholson, 2007), p. 201. This anecdote also provides another nuanced way of understanding Mirren's/Tennison's propensity to touch in the series.

62 *Prime Suspect: Behind the Scenes*.

63 Hayward and Rennert, *Prime Suspect: The Official Book of the Award-Winning Series*, p. 9.

64 Ibid., p. 14.

65 Ibid., p. 13. In fact, though set in London previous series had also actually been filmed in Manchester and Mirren felt it was time to use the city's own 'personality and character'. The final two instalments were both shot on location in London. The sense of place becomes far more embedded in these last three series, which make much use of landmarks and the urban environment, and incorporate a good deal of exterior and night-time shooting in the city's streets.

66 Neil Midgley, 'How Mirren Saved Tennison's Life', *Daily Telegraph*, 28 October 2006, p. 3.

67 *Prime Suspect: Behind the Scenes.*

68 Geoffrey Philips, review of *Trial and Retribution*, *Evening Standard*, 16 October 1997, p. 20.

69 Midgley, 'How Mirren Saved Tennison's Life', p. 3.

70 Ibid.

71 Hermione Eyre, review of *Prime Suspect: The Final Act*, *Independent on Sunday*, 22 October 2006, p. 18.

72 Anon., 'A Drama Queen', *Metro*, 16 October 2006, p. 27.

73 Libby Brooks, 'Past Her Prime', *Guardian*, 23 October 2006, available at <commentisfree.guardian.co.uk/libby_ brooks/2006/10/post_536.html> (accessed 31 October 2006).

74 'Freepoland', for example, pointed out that 'She solved the crime, ending a successful career on a high note', and observed 'I didn't find the end depressing … . Choices or sacrifices have to be made to get to the top in any profession and it is usually more difficult for women. A tv series that priodes (sic) itself on it's (sic) realism should reflect that situation'. Ibid., comment no. 266176.

75 Ibid., comment no. 266908.

76 Ibid., comment no. 266540.

77 Ibid., comment no. 266317.

78 Lynda La Plante in interview with Natasha Cooper.

79 Beth Hale, 'Lynda La Plante's Fury over Alcoholic Final Act for *Prime Suspect*', *Daily*

Mail, 20 October 2006, available at <www.dailymail.co.uk/tvshowbiz/article-411694/Lynda-La-Plantes-fury-alcoholic-final-act-Prime-Suspect.html> (accessed 31 October 2006).

80 Angela Bromstad, NBC Primetime President, cited in Michael Schneider, 'NBC Plans *Prime Suspect* Remake', *Variety*, 2 September 2009, available at <www.variety.com/article/VR1118008061. html?categoryid=1236&cs=1> (accessed 12 October 2009).

81 For example, in summer 2008 the UK's *Guardian* newspaper reported that a review of accredited forensic-science programmes in the US had found an estimated 75 per cent of graduates were now women. The piece continues:

> In [Virginia Commonwealth University's] forensic-science program, 33 women and 11 men finished the undergraduate program this year and 20 women and two men graduated from the graduate program. 'Women are the future of forensic science', said program director Bill Eggleston … 'It's not just evolving, it's a revolution.'

West Virginia University's Professor Max Houck is cited suggesting that the success and proliferation of women forensic investigators in television drama has been instrumental in this change. See Dena Potter, 'More Women Choosing Careers in Forensic Science', *Guardian*, 15 August 2008, available at <www.guardian.co.uk/ uslatest/story/0,,-7727371,00.html> (accessed 9 October 2008).

82 La Plante has said that the most important thing *Prime Suspect* might have achieved is to change the way the public feel about women heading a murder inquiry. In interview with Natasha Cooper.

Resources

(Current in October 2008)

US Masterpiece Theatre site featuring case studies of each *Prime Suspect* miniseries with synopses and cast and crew credits, plus a range of related web links including biographies of Mirren and La Plante and interviews on National Public Radio: <www.pbs.org/wgbh/masterpiece/ primesuspect>.

Watch the first two series of *Prime Suspect* and selected clips on ITV's website: <www.itv.com/ClassicTVshows/crime/ PrimeSuspect/default.html>.

BFI site providing a synopsis of the first *Prime Suspect*, cast and crew credits and links to other crime series. Clips and episodes can be viewed by registered schools/universities/libraries: <www.screenonline.org.uk/tv/id/493056/ index.html>.

Credits

Prime Suspect

created by
Lynda La Plante
production companies
Series one
Granada Television
Series two–seven
Granada Television and WGBH
(US)
broadcast history
Broadcast in the UK on
ITV/ITV1 in seven miniseries
between 7 April 1991 and 22
October 2006, a total of 15 x
2-hour episodes

Prime Suspect
part one tx 07/04/1991
part two tx 08/04/1991
director
Christopher Menaul
writer
Lynda La Plante
producer
Sally Head (executive
producer)
Don Leaver (producer)
co-ordinator
Sue Whitley
production manager
David Meddick
location manager
Lynne Marriott
assistant director (1st)
David Weir
assistant director (2nd)
Tania Normand
continuity
Hilda Miller
casting director
Doreen Jones
script associate
Jenny Sheridan
director of photography
Ken Morgan
camera operator
Howard Somers

Focus
David Bell
Graham Hazard
grip
Bob Gregory
Steadicam
Alf Tamontin
lighting gaffer
Jim Camp
graphic designer
Peter Terry
film editor
Edward Mansell
production designer
Roy Stonehouse
design assistant
Chris Stevenson
production buyer
Trevor Devoy
chargehand
Tony Mills
costume designer
Sheelagh Killeen
wardrobe supervisor
Anthony Black
make-up supervisor
Jane Hatch
make-up assistant
Tracey Dilly
prosthetics
Mike Moustafi
Colin Ware
music
Stephen Warbeck
sound mixer
Ray French
boom operator
Ian Hills
dubbing editor
David Rees
Simon Walton
Paul Griffiths-Davies
John Rutherford
dubbing mixer
Brian Saunders

cast
Helen Mirren
DCI Jane Tennison
Tom Bell
DS Bill Otley
John Benfield
DCS Michael Kernan
John Bowe
George Marlow
Bryan Pringle
Felix Norman
Zoë Wanamaker
Moyra Henson
Tom Wilkinson
Peter Rawlins
John Forgeham
DCI John Shefford
Craig Fairbrass
DI Frank Burkin
Jack Ellis
DI Tony Muddyman
Mossie Smith
WPC Maureen Havers
Ian Fitzgibbon
DC Jones
Andrew Tiernan
DC Rosper
Philip Wright
DC Lillie
Richard Hawley
DC Haskons
Mark Spalding
DC Oakhill
Dave Bond
DC Eastel
Terry Taplin
Commander Trayner
Gareth Tudor Price
Willy Chang
Andrew Abrahams
Tilly
Fionnuala Ellwood
Joyce
Maria Mescki
Martin Reeve
John Ireland
lab assistant
Francesca Ryan
Marianne

Jeremy Warder
Joey
Michael Fleming
Major Howard
Daphne Neville
Mrs Howard
Julie Sumnall
Karen
Ralph Fiennes
Michael
Wilfred Harrison
Mr Tennison
Noël Dyson
Mrs Tennison
Jessica Turner
Pam
Anna Savva
Mrs Salbanna
James Snell
Arnold Upcher
Malcolm Raeburn
Inspector Sleeth
Peter Dennis
toastmaster
Anthony Havering
barman
Mark Anthony Newman
Doctor Lambton
Brian Hayes
TV presenter
Sandra Butterworth
WPC 'Karen'
Vincent Pickering
witness
Bryonie Pritchard
WPC Southwood
Barbara Dryhirst
WPC Raeburn
Anthony Schaeffer
uniformed driver

Prime Suspect 2
part one tx 15/12/1992
part two tx 16/12/1992
director
John Strickland
writer
Allan Cubitt (story by Lynda La Plante)
producer
Sally Head (executive producer)
Paul Marcus (producer)
production manager
David Meddick

1st assistant
Ian Galley
location manager
Ken Mair
continuity
Sue Wild
camera operator
Howard Somers
focus
David Bell
clapper loader
Steve Brooks
grips
Mike Fisher
Mike Heaney
sound recordist
Nick Steer
boom operators
Tony Cooper
David Eve
dubbing editors
Jaquie Ophir
John Senior
dubbing mixer
John Whitworth
gaffer
Jimmy Camp
chargehand
Tony Mills
props
Terry Nixon
graphics
Mark Nuttall
assistant designer
David Butterworth
2nd assistant
Rochelle Broman
production buyer
Trevor Devoy
costume designer
Mike O'Neill
wardrobe supervisor
Anne Rudd
make-up supervisor
Jane Hatch
make-up assistant
Linda Strath
co-ordinator
Milly Preece
script editor
Catriona McKenzie

cast
Helen Mirren
DCI Tennison

Colin Salmon
DS Oswalde
John Benfield
Det Supt Kernan
Jack Ellis
DI Muddyman
Philip Wright
DC Lillie
Richard Hawley
DI Haskons
Craig Fairbrass
DI Burkin
Andrew Tiernan
DC Rosper
Ian Fitzgibbon
DC Jones
Dev Sagoo
Mr Vishwandha
Stephen Boxer
DCI Thorndike
Jenny Jules
Sarah Allen
Fraser James
Tony Allen
Tom Watson
David Harvey
Corinne Skinner-Carter
Nola
Adrian Schiller
Gold
David Ryall
Oscar Bream
Shireen Shah
Mrs Vinwandha
Stephan Kalipha
Jonathan Phelps
Burt Caesar
Patterson
Claire Benedict
Esme Allen
Junior Laniyan
David Allen
Ashley James
Cleo Allen
Nina Sosanya
murdered girl

Prime Suspect 3
part one tx 19/12/1993
part two tx 20/12/1993
director
David Drury
writer
Lynda La Plante

121

producer
Sally Head (executive
producer)
Lynda La Plante (associate
producer)
Paul Marcus (producer)
production executive
Craig McNeil
production co-ordinator
Milly Preece
production manager
David Weddick
location manager
Jeff Bowen
assistant director
Vinny Fahy
script supervisor
Sue Wild
casting director
Doreen Jones
script editor
Valery Ryan
script associate
Gwenda Bagshaw
DOP
David Odd
camera operator
Howard Somers
focus puller
David Bell
camera grips
Mike Fisher
gaffer
Jimmy Camp
graphic designer
Mark Nuttall
film editor
Edward Mansell
production designer
Chris Truelove
art director
Tom Brown
props
Simon Dalton
costume designer
Mike O'Neill
wardrobe supervisor
Anne Rudd
make-up supervisor
Jane Hatch
make-up assistant
Margaret O'Keefe
music
Stephen Warbeck

sound mixer
Nick Steer
camera grips
David Eve
re-recording mixer
John Whitworth
Andy Wyatt
dubbing editor
Jackie Ophis
John Senior
stunt co-ordinator
Terry Forrestal

cast
Helen Mirren
DCI Tennison
Tom Bell
Sgt Bill Otley
Peter Capaldi
Vera Reynolds
David Thewlis
Jimmy Jackson
Ciarán Hinds
Edward Parker-Jones
Kelly Hunter
Jessica Smithy
Terrence Hardiman
Commander Chiswick
Struan Rodger
Supt Halliday
Mark Strong
Insp Larry Hall
Liza Sadovy
WPC Norma Hastings
Andrew Woodall
DI Brian Dalton
Richard Hawley
DS Richard Haskons
Philip Wright
DC Lillie
Mark Drewry
DI Ray Hebdon
Christopher Fairbank
Chief Insp David Lyall
Michael J. Shannon
Jake Hunter
Olive Pendleton
Mrs Field
Jonny Lee Miller
Anthony Field
Andrew Dicks
Billy Matthews
Pearce Quigley
Red

Richard Cadman
Alan Thorpe
James Frain
Jason Baldwin
John Blakey
Brian
Felix Bell
Rutter
Alyson Spiro
Margaret Speel
John Axon
Jackson's lawyer
John Benfield
Chief Supt Kernan
Terence Harvey
John Kenningon
Rowena Cooper
Mrs Kennington
Paul Aspden
Kenny Lloyd
Brian Spink
Parker-Jones's lawyer
Kaye James
WPC Bronwen
Jeremy Golton
Disco Driscoll
David Gambles
Frankie
Robin Polley
club MC
Mark Pepper
police officer
Kelly Derbyshire
girl at station
Danny Dyer
Martin Fletcher

*Prime Suspect 4: The Lost
Child*
tx 30/04/1995
director
John Madden
writer
Paul Billing
producer
Rebecca Eaton (executive
producer: USA)
Sally Head (executive
producer)
Paul Marcus (producer)
production executive
Craig McNeil
production finance
Carl Morris

production co-ordinator
Milly Preece
casting director
Doreen Jones
script editor
Valery Ryan
Elizabeth Bradley
script associate
Gwenda Bagshaw
DOP
David Odd
gaffer
Jimmy Camp
special effects
Steve Tomkow
graphic designer
Murray Cook
film editor
Anthony Ham
production designer
Chris Truelove
art director
Stephen Graham
assistant art director
Iain Andrews
s/b props
Terry Nixon
production buyer
Trevor Devoy
construction manager
Tony Mills
costume designer
Mike O'Neill
wardrobe supervisor
Samantha Horn
make-up supervisor
Jane Hatch
make-up assistant
Anastasia Shirley
music
Stephen Warbeck
sound mixer
Nick Steer
dubbing editor
John Rutherford
John Senior
boom operator
Ben Brooke
re-recording mixer
Dean Humphries
stunt co-ordinator
Andy Bradford

cast
Helen Mirren
Jane Tennison
Beatie Edney
Susan Covington
Robert Glenister
Chris Hughes
Lesley Sharp
Anne Sutherland
John Benfield
Chief Supt Kernan
Richard Hawley
DI Haskons
Jack Ellis
DI Muddyman
David Phelan
DI Pride
Tony Rohr
DS McColl
Mark Bazeley
DC Aplin
Mossie Smith
WPC Havers
Caroline Selby
Alison Sutherland
Candice Paul
Gayle Sutherland
Adrian Links
John Warwick
Fergus O'Donnell
DC Hawker
Stuart Wilson
Dr Patrick Schofield
Steve Tindall
DCI White
David Ryall
Oscar Bream
Patrick Cremin
DI Andrews
Sam Cox
DCI Birnam
Richard Cubison
Commander Lane
Mac Andrews
Stubbs
Malcolm Raeburn
Supt Sleeth

Prime Suspect 4: Inner Circles
tx 07/05/1995
director
Sarah Pia Anderson
writer
Eric Deacon (story by Meredith Oakes)

producer
Rebecca Eaton (executive producer: USA)
Sally Head (executive producer)
Paul Marcus (producer)
production supervisor
Bill Leather
production manager
David Meddick
assistant director (1st)
Vincent Fahy
assistant director (2nd)
Sue Whitley
location manager
David Weir
continuity
Sue Wild
camera operator
Howard Somers
focus
Craig Feather
clapperloader
Tony Ling
camera grips
Mike Fisher
sound mixer
Nick Steer
boom operator
David Eve
dubbing editors
John Rutherford
John Senior
re-recording mixer
John Whitworth
gaffer
Jimmy Camp
construction manager
Tony Mills
s/b props
Terry Nixon
graphic designer
Murray Cook
art director
Claire Kenny
assistant art director
Iain Andrews
production buyer
Trevor Devoy
production finance
Carl Morris
costume designer
Mike O'Neill
wardrobe supervisor
Samantha Horn

123

make-up supervisor
Kathy Ducker
make-up assistant
Samantha Print
production co-ordinator
Milly Preece
stunt co-ordinator
Jim Dowdall
special effects
Steve Tomkow
script editors
Elizabeth Bradley
Valery Ryan
script associate
Gwenda Bagshaw

cast
Helen Mirren
Supt Jane Tennison
Jill Baker
Maria Henry
Helene Kvale
Lynne Endicott
Kelly Reilly
Polly Henry
Gareth Forwood
Denis Carradine
Phillada Sewell
Olive Carradine
Jonathan Copestake
Micky Thomas
Julie Rice
Sheila Bower
Roger Milner
old man
Sam Rumbelow
PC Wilson
Ralph Arliss
DCI Raymond
Sophie Stanton
DS Cromwell
Thomas Craig
DS Booth
Christopher John Hall
DC Bakari
James Kerr
DC Lee
Richard Hawley
DI Haskons
Nick Patrick
Hamish Carradine
Ian Flintoff
Supt Mallory
John Benfield
Chief Supt Kernan

Alan Perrin
Derek Palmer
Myles Hoyle
Mr Brant
Michael Stainton
George

Prime Suspect 4: The Scent of Darkness
tx 15/05/1995
director
Paul Marcus
writer
Guy Hibbert
producer
Rebecca Eaton (executive producer: USA)
Sally Head (executive producer)
Brian Park (producer)
production executive
Craig McNeill
production supervisor
Bill Leather
production buyer
Trevor Devoy
production finance
Carl Morris
production co-ordinator
Milly Preece
production manager
David Meddick
location manager
David Weir
continuity
Sue Wild
assistant director (1st)
Vincent Fahy
Assistant director (2nd)
Sue Debouvoir
casting director
Doreen Jones
script editor
Valery Ryan
Elizabeth Bradshaw
script associate
Gwenda Bagshaw
DOP
David Odd
camera operator
Howard Somers
focus puller
Craig Feather
clapperloader
Tony Ling

camera grips
Mike Fisher
gaffer
Jimmy Camp
graphic designer
Murray Cook
film editor
Edward Mansell
production designer
Chris Truelove
art director
Claire Kenny
assistant art director
Iain Andrews
s/b props
Terry Nixon
construction manager
Tony Mills
costume designer
Mike O'Neill
wardrobe supervisor
Samantha Horn
make-up supervisor
Jane Hatch
make-up assistant
Margaret O'Keefe
music
Stephen Warbeck
sound mixer
Nick Steer
boom operator
Martin Beresford
re-recording mixer
John Whitworth
dubbing editor
John Rutherford
John Senior
stunt co-ordinator
Andy Bradford

cast
Helen Mirren
Supt Jane Tennison
Tim Woodward
George Marlow
Stephen Boxer
Supt David Thorndike
Christopher Fulford
DCI Tom Mitchell
Alan Leith
Supt Howell
Hugh Simon
Chief Inspector Finlay
Stuart Wilson
Dr Patrick Schofield

Penelope Beaumont
Dr Elizabeth Bramwell
Richard Hawley
DI Richard Haskons
Christopher Ashley
Anthony Bramwell
Pip Donaghy
Len Sheldon
Glen Berry
Wayne
Joseph Kpobie
Al
Otis Munyang'iri
Pete
Rebecca Thorn
policewoman 1
Scott Neal
Geoff
Martin Stone
1st prisoner
Mark Phoenix
2nd prisoner
Marc Warren
DC Andy Dyson
Antony Byrne
DC Jason Headley
Andreas Markos
Takis Hulenkinis
Darrell D'Silva
Andreas Hulenkinis
Tanya Ronder
WPC Lawford
Stafford Gordon
Commander Trayner
Ray Fearon
Mark Whitehouse
Sam Halpenny
Bill Douglas
Linda Henry
forensic scientist
David Ryall
Oscar Bream
John Benfield
Chief Supt Kernan
Caroline Strong
DC Catherine Cooper
Geoffrey Church
DS Colin Blake
Nick Miles
TV interviewer
Sadie Shimmin
Mrs Williams
Karen Salt
Kate Matthews

Jason Cheater
policewoman
Lara Harvey
policewoman 2
Heather Emmanuel
nurse
Kate Ashfield
helper
Joyce Redman
Doris Marlow
Ruth Carraway
Kelly
Elaine Lordon
Tracy
Tim Wallers
motorist
Dermot Keaney
Raymond Harding

Prime Suspect 5: Errors of
Judgement
part one tx 20/10/1996
part two tx 21/10/1996
director
Philip Davis
writer
Guy Andrews
producer
Rebecca Eaton (executive
producer: USA)
Gub Neal (executive producer)
Lynn Horsford (producer)
Nicola Schindler (associate
producer)
production executive
Craig McNeil
production supervisor
Bill Leather
production manager
Des Hughes
location manager
Josh Dynevor
script editor
Rachel Bennette
DOP
Barry McCann
film editor
Anthony Ham
designer
Chris Truelove
music
Stephen Warbeck
sound mixer
Phil Smith

cast
Helen Mirren
Supt Jane Tennison
John McArdle
Ballinger
Julia Lane
Devanney
David O'Hara
Rankine
John Brobbey
Henry Adeliyeka
Steven Mackintosh
The Street
Ray Emmett Brown
Michael Johns
Paul Oldham
Toots
Joe Speare
Radio
Paul Simpson
Outboard
Joseph Jacobs
Campbell Lafferty
Marsha Thomson
Janice
Vanessa Knox-Mawer
Louise Ballinger
Badi Uzzman
Mr Ahmed
Anne Hornby
DC Skinner
Steve Money
desk sergeant
Chris Bisson
Nazir
Anthony Audenshaw
DC Growse
Gabrielle Reidy
Noreen Lafferty
Sarah Jones
Deborah Pagett
Ravin Gannattra
Mooz
David Webber
Rector
Martin Ronan
Pardy
Adam Evans
photographer
Julian Kerridge
young doctor
Emma Longbottom
Pree
Andy Devine
grave-faced reporter

125

Stuart Wolfenden
cheeky reporter
David Kangas
Poyser
Dave Norman
Tony Rice

Prime Suspect 6: The Last Witness
part one tx 09/11/2003
part two tx 10/11/2003
director
Tom Hooper
writer
Peter Berry
producer
Rebecca Eaton (executive producer: USA)
Andy Harries (executive producer)
David Boulter (producer)
Thea Harvey (line producer)
assistant director (1st)
Matthew Carver
assistant director (2nd)
Paul Mason
runner
Nicola Parfitt
stand-in
Helen Slaymaker
location manager
Andrew Macdonald-Brown
unit manager
Michelle Pianca
location assistant
Harriet Griffin
production co-ordinator
Mhairi Brennan
production secretary
Eve Petcher
production runner
Alex Hodgson
script supervisor
Cathy Doubleday
production accountant
Adrian O'Brian
assistant accountant
Kerry Bates
casting assistant
Liz Vincent-Ferne
additional casting
Stephanie Dawes
art director
Niall Moroney

standby art director
Penny Harvey
art department assistant
Caroline Barclay
production buyer
Marshall Aver
property master
Gary Watson
standby props
Kevin Scarrott
Mark Brooks
dressing props
Andy Mortimer
Andy Harris
construction manager
Rob Anderson
standby carpenter
Will Pope
standby painter
Jonathan Holbrook
rigger
Dave Bayliss
camera operator
Martin Foley
focus puller
Matt Wesson
clapperloader
Ray Meer
camera trainee
Chris Williams
video playback operator
Ossie Bacon
grip
Ronan Murphy
Steadicam operators
Roger Tooley
Andrei Austin
2nd unit camera operator
Gary Spratling
David Shillingford
2nd unit focus puller
Jon Webb
Ralph Ramsden
2nd unit clapperloader
Sophie Wilson
additional sound recordist
Sandy Macrae
sound maintenance
Jeremy Lishman
sound assistant
Delta Okin
Caroline Colman
assistant costume designer
Nigel Egerton

costume supervisor
Amanda Harward
wardrobe supervisor
Phil Goldsworthy
wardrobe trainee
Nadine Powell
make-up artists
Sharon O'Brien
Claire Whiteley
make-up trainee
Kristina Roberts
stunt co-ordinators
Paul Heasman
Lee Sheward
Andy Bradford
Gareth Milne
Elaine Ford
technical advisors
Sue Akers
David Bright
Lara Carmel
Steve Duffy
Simon Geoghegan
Vuleta Jocic
Norman McKinley
Rosslyn Rankin
Neem Visavidia
John Yates
unit nurse
Carol Hutchinson
press and publicity
Holly Palin
Patrick Smith
Simone le Lievre
assistant editor
Natasha Wilkinson
online editors
Simon Giblin
Shane Warden
Telecine colourist
Adam Scott
music programming
Mike Trim
dialogue editor
Nick Roberts
effects editor
Sean O'Shea
dubbing mixer
Ben Baird
casting director
Doreen Jones
line producer
Thea Harvey
production executive
Gary Connelly

126

head of production
Marigo Kehoe
script editors
Jenny Grayn
Roberto Troni
assistant director (1st)
Stephen Woolfenden
sound recordist
Simon Okin
make-up designer
David Myers
costume designer
Annie Symons
composer
Rob Lane
film editor
St John O'Rorke
production designer
Claire Kenny
DOP
Larry Smith

cast
Helen Mirren
Det Supt Jane Tennison
Ben Miles
DCI Simon Finch
Barnaby Kay
DC Michael Phillips
Robert Pugh
DS Alun Simms
Mark Strong
Det Chief Supt Larry Hall
Tony Pritchard
DAC Charles Evans
Tanya Moodie
DC Lorna Greaves
Sam Hazeldine
DC David Butcher
Velibor Topic
Duscan Aigic
Oleg Men'shikov
Milan Lukic
Femi Oguns
Stephen Abacha
Ingeborga Dapkunaite
Jasmina Blekic
Liam Cunningham
Robert West
Leena Dhingra
pathologist
Steve Gibbs
DC Sean Firth
Ann Warungu
Haweeya

Rad Lazar
Kasim Ibranimivic
Kate Lynn-Evans
Rosemary Henderson
Bharti Patel
Tennison's secretary
Alex Giannini
custody sergeant
Dennis Titus
landlord
Stuart Goodwin
Anthony Vane
Sally Hirst
OCB secretary
Hugh Sachs
Boris Stone
Anna Maria Ashe
newsreader
Rupert Frazer
George Giblin MP
Finlay Robertson
Waterloo vagrant
Clare Holman
Elizabeth Likic
Frank Finlay
Arnold Tennison
Phoebe Nichols
Shaw
Serge Soric
optician
Nadia Cameron-Blakey
Sarah Ford
Davyd Harries
Lukic's solicitor
Valentine Pelka
SO19 Commander
Adna Sabljic
Serbian woman
Boris Boskovic
angry Serbian man
Aleksandar Mikic
hotel clerk
Etela Pardo
filing clerk
Dado Jehan
Bosnian gunman
Olegar Fedoro
Muslim man at docks

Prime Suspect: The Final Act
part one tx 15/10/2006
part two tx 22/10/2006
director
Philip Martin

writer
Frank Deasy
producer
Rebecca Eaton (executive
producer: USA)
Andy Harries (executive
producer)
Andrew Benson (producer)
Claudine Sturdy (line producer)
location manager
Ian Pollington
casting director
Doreen Jones
DOP
Julian Court
film editor
Trevor Waite
production designer
Candida Otton
costume designer
Joanna Eatwell
costume supervisor
Joanna Macklin
make-up designer
Deanne Turner
make-up
Isabelle Webley
hair
Deanne Turner
composer
Nicholas Hooper
music
Karen Turner
sound recording
Chris Ashworth
dubbing
Paul Hamblin
Becki Ponting
stunt co-ordinator
Andreas Petrides

cast
Helen Mirren
DSI Jane Tennison
Stephen Tompkinson
Sean Phillips
Laura Greenwood
Penny Phillips
Eve Best
Linda Phillips
Katy Murphy
Ruth Sturdy
Gary Lewis
Tony Sturdy

127

Frank Finlay
Arnold Tennison
Robert Pugh
DS Simms
Brendan Coyle
DCS Mitchell
Robbie Gee
DI Traynor
Russell Mabey
Cox
Heshima Thompson
Curtis
Laura Doddington
DC Wood
Tom Bell
Bill Otley
Carolyn Pickles
Pauline
Maxine Barton
Sallie Sturdy
Amanda Crichlow
Gloria

Sharon Maharaj
consultant
Clive Hayward
pathologist
Ricky Nixon
Lester
Seroca Davis
Delores
Amanda Wright
Vanessa
Lakechia Jeanne
Destiny
Ellie Kendrick
Melanie
Badria Timimi
Curtis's lawyer
Iain Mitchell
Sean's lawyer
Ashley Madekwe
Tanya
Nonso Anozie
Robert

Lee Whitlock
Jeremy
Sydney White
girl on heath
Dystin Johnson
staff nurse (night)
Rebecca Clay
staff nurse (day)
Ronnie Fox
barman
Olivia Lumley
Carol
Tim Preece
AA main speaker
David Keyes
AA top table
Alex Blake
Ray
Helen Griffin
female AA speaker

Index

Also Published: